· Conservation and La

# Conservation and · Land Use ·

**Karen V Jones**
LLB, LLM
*Solicitor*

*Foreword by*
**Richard Macrory**
Professor of Environmental Law
University College, London

Palladian Law Publishing Ltd

© Karen Jones
2000

Published by
Palladian Law Publishing Ltd
Beach Road
Bembridge
Isle of Wight
PO35 5NQ

www.palladianlaw.com

ISBN 1 902558 07 3

Typeset by Heath Lodge Publishing Services
Printed in Great Britain by The Cromwell Press Ltd

# · Contents ·

# · Foreword ·

This is a timely and well-judged book. The last decade has seen an explosion of publications concerned with UK environmental law, but compared with the intricacies of waste regulation, Integrated Pollution Control, contaminated land and the like, conservation law has remained something of a Cinderella amongst recent studies. Yet as Karen Jones demonstrates, conservation law permeates our relationship with the environment. It is vitally important to all those who have dealings with land and property.

Many areas of our national legal structures are now strongly influenced by European developments. Conservation law is no exception where a powerful web of EU legislation has been developed, backed up by some equally strong decisions of the European Court of Justice. These developments are all covered in this book.

Karen Jones has provided an accessible guide to the contemporary framework of laws which will prove invaluable to both the specialist and the uninitiated. She writes as someone with practical experience of the key issues and problem areas likely to be faced in dealing with this area of the law, and in a style that can be understood by both the lawyer and non-lawyer. Flow-diagrams and chapter summaries provide admirable route-maps through the complexities, and she deals with the latest Government policy proposals which will bring about further legal changes.

As we enter the new Millennium it is an appropriate time to reflect on the adequacy of our existing conservation laws, and the policies that underlie them. Why do we wish to conserve? What do we want to conserve? How are conservation needs balanced against potentially conflicting economic and social pressures? Law provides a key mechanism for reflecting and resolving these tensions, but the questions are ones that concern everyone.

This book provides the firm grounding for an informed debate.

Richard Macrory
Professor of Environmental Law
University College, London

# · Preface ·

I have been involved in environmental law from the very beginning of my career. I started to practise it as a discrete discipline when I took a position in the North Midlands. This proved to be a splendid geographical area for an environmental lawyer, with the legacy of past industrial uses providing some of the most challenging problems any lawyer is likely to face. The more environmental experience I gained, the more I became aware that "environment" and "environmental problems" were more often than not equated purely with the impact of pollution on the three environmental media of air, water and land. In the majority of environmental textbooks I consulted the discussion was restricted to what I thought should more correctly be described as "pollution law". Even where a work did deal with conservation, it was as a side issue to pollution control. Perhaps the absence of hard law in this area was the reason for it being a less pressing concern for landowners and their advisers. In recent years conservation issues have occupied a far higher profile. The Government has promised reform of the law and this seems to have been chiefly prompted by the public's increasing disquiet with the existing state of the law.

The omission of the law relating to conservation and landscape protection from discussions of environmental law presents an incomplete picture. This book has two major aims: to try to fill the gap caused by the omission of conservation issues from the majority of the works on environmental law and to provide the basic but comprehensive guidance required to be able to consider and advise on the law relating to conservation issues.

Conservation is a subject that is rarely out of the news these days. It is a matter of frequent discussion in the daily press and is fast becoming one of the most immediate environmental concerns. It is a topic that is of very obvious concern to the public and one on which the Government has promised action. It will undoubtedly be a matter for more careful and detailed consideration for landowners and their advisers in the near future. Recent months have seen promises of review on issues such as right to roam, improvement of SSSI protection and AONB designation. At the time of writing, no parliamentary time has been allocated for any legislation and some of the proposals for reform are based on improvement of administrative arrangements. This may mean that no greater conservation protections will arise as a result of the latest review and it must be questioned whether such an approach to reform can be effective in improving the protective regime. Many would hope that a complete overhaul of the system will come about, although the legislature missed the most appropriate opportunity for this in years at the time the Habitats Directive was implemented into UK law. It would seem that conservation law reform is likely to be a slow process.

This book is intended to be an easy reference work for those unfamiliar with conservation law and to assist practitioners who have some knowledge but need to be able to refer to the detail at any given time. The drawback of the present regime is that there is less hard law than one would expect but I hope to have covered all the potential difficulties that may arise in connection with a nature conservation designation. This book will also be a helpful reference for those who are fortunate and privileged enough to occupy a site subject to a local or national nature conservation designation.

I should thank many more people than can be named here for their involvement and help while I was writing this book. The superb coverage of conservation issues by Donald McGillvary during my LLM studies some years ago fired a particular interest in this area of environmental law. My friends, Laura Devine and Helen Parker, provided support and encouragement as well as practical help over the time I have been engaged on this project. My husband, Mike, provided the technology and lessons on how to use it! This book is dedicated to him. Thanks are also due to Palladian Law Publishing who have guided me through the writing process and for their patience in waiting for the finished text.

The law is stated as at 31 July 1999. Any mistakes are entirely my own. I would welcome any comments on the book.

Karen Jones
Barton-under-Needwood
1 November 1999

# · Table of Cases ·

# · Table of Statutes ·

# Table of Statutory Instruments

# · Table of EU Directives ·

| Birds | Directive | (79/409/EEC) |
|---|---|---|
| | 15, 21, 23, 24, 28, 33, 40 | |
| Art 1 | | 16, 17 |
| Art 2 | | 16, 17, 19, 20 |
| Art 3 | | 16 |
| Art 4 | | 16, 17, 20 |
| Arts 5-9 | | 16 |
| Annex I | | 16, 17, 20, 25 |

| Habitats | Directive | (92/43/EEC) |
|---|---|---|
| | 11, 15, 20, 21, 24, 33, 40, 59, 74, | |
| | 88, 119 | |
| Art 4 | | 22 |
| Art 5 | | 22 |
| Art 6 | | 19, 23 |
| Annex I | | 27, 28 |
| Annex II | | 27, 28 |
| Annex III | | 22 |

# · Abbreviations ·

| | |
|---|---|
| AONB | area of outstanding natural beauty |
| CA | Countryside Act 1968 |
| CSS | Country Stewardship Scheme |
| DDP | Director of Public Prosecutions |
| ECJ | European Court of Justice |
| EPA | Environmental Protection Act 1990 |
| ESA | environmentally sensitive area |
| GPDO | general permitted development order |
| IPC | integrated pollution control |
| LPA | local planning authority |
| MAFF | Ministry of Agriculture, Fisheries and Food |
| MNR | marine nature reserve |
| NCC | Nature Conservancy Council |
| NCO | nature conservation order |
| NNR | national nature reserve |
| NP | national park |
| NPA | national parks authority |
| NPACA | National Parks and Access to the Countryside Act 1949 |
| PDO | potentially damaging operation |
| PPG | government planning policy guidance note |
| RSPB | Royal Society for the Protection of Birds |
| SAC | special area of conservation |
| SNCO | special nature conservation order |
| SPA | special protection area |
| SSSI | site of special scientific interest |
| TCPA | Town and Country Planning Act 1990 |
| WCA | Wildlife and Countryside Act 1981 |

*Chapter 1*

# Legislative Framework and · Bodies Charged with · Conservation Duties

## *1.1* Growth of nature conservation protections

### The historic context

Conservation law has a fairly recent history in the United Kingdom. Some conservation measures have been in place for very many years, but the purpose of the legislative framework has only recently changed. Conservation law has its history in a "value to human beings" philosophy, a way of conserving things, not for the sake of conservation, but for the value they represent to human beings who may be able to exploit the conservation for their own advantage. Legal controls were introduced on an *ad hoc* basis not for the protection of the environment itself but on a value to human beings basis, so that the protection of a habitat or species of game, for example, was an incidental benefit of the human centred approach to conservation. An example of this type of conservation has been in existence for many years for the protection of game birds. The "closed season" for shooting, during which hunting for certain types of game bird is prohibited, ensures that the shooting season itself is all the more profitable because there is ample game to kill. The law has also been utilised as a mechanism to address a particular problem. Large elements of protection arose from legislation not to conserve, which was an unintended bonus, but to stop cruelty or protect individual species from a particular trade, for example to stop the feather trade for use in the fashion industry.

### Modern-day conservation

It is now accepted that conservation needs to be seen as a factor for consideration in all decision-making equations, and that the original *ad hoc* approach to conservation cannot continue. The general public now demands that nature conservation and environment considerations are taken into account to enhance everyday life. It is accepted in modern conservation thinking that there is little point in conserving increasingly isolated areas of countryside for their natural beauty without taking into account nature conservation considerations in the general round of decision-making. This new approach to conservation issues means that nature conservation concerns will be more prominent in decision-making and will frequently come into conflict with traditional property rights and with the rights of individuals to use and exploit land and natural resources.

**Future developments**

Nature conservation is today a politically topical subject. With increasing evidence that the loss of diversity of nature influences the balance of the very planet we occupy, there is more pressure than ever for increased conservation measures. This means increased weight for the consideration of environmental effects in the decision-making process. One of the central problems with conservation and a factor which has to date hampered nature conservation objectives is the fact that conservation measures are long term and often require draconian short-term measures to ensure their success. In the political arena, long-term measures are not always welcome: long-term commitments do little to influence short-term voting habits. Governments are often reluctant to commit to the necessary long- term measures and the resources those measures may entail, which may be vital to conservation. The international forum clearly demonstrates these difficulties - the efforts to combat world-wide conservation issues such as the biodiversity of the planet or the protection of individual endangered species have proved extremely difficult for states to negotiate and agree. The law of conservation might be said to still be in its infancy, and it seems inevitable that pressures will continue to grow for increased long-term regulation and enforced conservation measures. This will result in more landowners being subject to nature conservation measures and in turn an increasing demand that they forego their own individual rights for the good of the conservation objective.

## 1.2 **Overview of effect of nature conservation designations**

It is possible, and in the case of valuable sites usual, for the same site to carry a number of designations, with differing rules and protection, at the same time. The use of designations is often cumulative so that a "layering" of different protection may apply to a piece of land. This means that a single piece of land may attract differing protection and as a result various penalties for non-compliance with those protections. This can be confusing for layperson and practitioner alike. Any such designation means that the owner or occupier of the land is not entirely at liberty to do as he or she wishes on the land without hindrance or administrative burden. The general effects of designation could be all or any of the following:

(1) Permission should be obtained for activities that a landowner would normally carry out as a matter of right. This could be labelled an interference with the owner's ordinary property rights.
(2) The fact of designation may be a material consideration of any application for planning permission in respect of the land. This is a natural consequence of the fact that planning permission will override any nature conservation designation.
(3) If an area of land is subject to the highest nature conservation designations made under the Conservation (Natural Habitats, etc) Regulations 1994, planning permission must not be granted in most circumstances unless there are "imperative reasons of overriding public interest" or considerations of human health and safety. This means that the owner of land subject to such a designation will need an exceptional case for planning permission if the planning proposal will have any effect on the site's integrity (for a definition of which see p 119 below).
(4) The fact of designation will be recorded as a local land charge and should as a result be known to any potential purchaser of any part of the land subject to the designation.
(5) Not only will a landowner be unable to exercise all of his normal property rights, but he may also be obliged by a management agreement imposed on the land to carry out certain positive obligations.
(6) Compensation may be payable for agricultural or forestry activities which cannot be carried out as a direct result of the designation or limitations which reduce the land's commercial return.

(7) As land worth conserving becomes more scarce, a landowner may find his or her land subject to an additional designation (*e.g.* from a site of special scientific interest (SSSI) to a candidate special area of conservation (SAC) or special protection area (SPA) which imposes stricter restrictions or greater penalties. This could occur not because of any intrinsic additional value of the land but because of the increased public demands for continued conservation.

(8) Failure to adhere to the requirements of the nature conservation regime governing land and the procedures it imposes (*e.g.* to give notice of the intention to carry out certain activities) may result in the commission of a criminal offence.

## *1.3* **Problems and difficulties**

Many landowners have lived on and worked land subject to a nature conservation designation without that designation unduly restricting their activities. This is in many cases still the case and will probably continue to be so for the majority of them. It is a historic fact that most sites subject to nature conservation designations were in the ownership of very few landowners. In the present climate for conservation this situation is sure to change, because more designations are likely to be made to meet increasing demands for conservation of the natural environment. Designations are likely for smaller parcels of land, which will mean that nature conservation designations in various forms will have an effect on an increasing number of landowners. It is my view that these will become an important consideration for those who seek to live and work on or develop such land. Problems and difficulties will invariably arise.

### **Problems arising from designation**

These might include:

(1) restrictions on the use to which an owner may put the land;

(2) difficulty in overcoming policy objections to obtain planning permission for development or operations to be carried out on the land

(3) restrictions on any permitted development rights which might be available to the owner or occupier of land;

(4) the increased risk to a landowner of committing a criminal offence

(because an operation on the land is carried out in breach of any list of potentially damaging operations in force in respect of the land); and

(5) the added burden, in some cases, of the necessity of managing the land for nature conservation purposes; obligations may be imposed by means of a management agreement in force in respect of the land, which will further restrict the landowner.

**Problems with the designation regime**

In addition the designation regime itself gives rise to a number of problems including:

(1) confusion because of the number of habitat protection designations in place about what particular protection a site attracts and what penalties or sanctions are available for breach of that protection;
(2) a failure to appreciate the distinction between nature conservation and public leisure and recreation - enjoyment of land by the general public is not necessarily compatible with conservation of it;
(3) the fact of legal protection does not in itself guarantee the conservation of a site; the effects of activities on neighbouring land or of external pollutants such as air-borne pollution will not be controlled under the regime; and
(4) the inability of the present regime to impose positive obligations to ensure conservation unless a voluntary management agreement is concluded - illustrated in *R v Nature Conservancy Council ex parte London Brick Property Ltd* [1996] Env LR 1 (see p 44 below).

## 1.4 Bodies responsible for nature conservation

### English Nature

An original nature conservancy body set up by Royal Charter in 1949 was the Nature Conservancy. This became a statutory body, the Nature Conservancy Council (NCC), under the Nature Conservancy Council Act 1973. This statutory body was established as a government body, independent of the various government departments, and fully autonomous. In the true tradition of a quango NCC members were appointed by the Secretaries of State. The NCC existed in this form until 1990. It seems that with increasing political interest in conservation issues the NCC was too powerful a body, which, in its role to protect nature conservation interests, hampered Government interests. The NCC had become particularly powerful in Scotland where it had opposed certain land use activities which attracted grant aid, such as the scheme proposed by Mr Cameron for afforestation in *Cameron* v *Nature Conservancy Council* (1992) 9207 EG 128, 9208 EG 120 and 9209 EG 147 (see Chap 4, pp 51-52). The NCC became a target for Government reform during the 1980s.

The reform came about by means of the Environment Act 1990 and took the form of a split of the original NCC. It was divided into three bodies responsible for separate geographical areas: the NCC for England, known (and referred to throughout this book) as "English Nature", the Countryside Council for Wales and the NCC for Scotland (later to become Scottish Natural Heritage). Consequently, many commentators said, the nature conservation influence in government decision-making was reduced as the original NCC's overall power lessened once divided. It is open to debate whether the potential for a reduction in power was a motivation for reform.

Section 128 of the Environment Protection Act (EPA) 1990 created the English and Welsh bodies ("the Councils"). This section originally applied to Scotland, but in this with respect was repealed by the Natural Heritage (Scotland) Act 1991. Sections 132 and 133 of EPA 1990 set out the Councils' functions, including:

- the establishment, maintenance and management of nature reserves;
- giving advice to the Secretary of State on the development and implementation of policies for or affecting nature conservation;
- giving advice and disseminating knowledge to any persons about nature conservation or matters arising from discharge of their functions;
- commissioning or supporting of research which in their opinion is relevant to their functions;
- establishing common standards throughout Great Britain to monitor nature conservation and for research into nature conservation; and
- the functions previously discharged by the NCC under the Wildlife and Countryside Act (WCA) 1981 as are assigned to the Councils under EPA 1990.

Section 133 also provides that the individual Councils shall have regard to any advice given to them by the Joint Nature Conservation Committee (see below). Subsection (3) enables the joint committee to give advice in connection with a council's functions where in the committee's opinion any matter concerns nature conservation for Great Britain as a whole.

Each of the three bodies receives a government grant. They are responsible, in particular, for the selection and management of National Nature Reserves (NNRs) and SSSIs. The power to establish nature reserves is in section 16 of the National Parks and Access to the Countryside Act (NPACA) 1949. Nature reserves are areas that the Councils will own or have complete control of. The Councils are also responsible for the designation of SSSIs under section 28 of WCA 1981 (see Chap 4), although SSSIs may be in the control of a third party. The Councils are the Government's statutory advisors on nature conservation issues and are statutory consultees in the planning process and for pollution control consents.

A body to take over the NCC's role in relation to the UK's international obligations was established as the Joint Nature Conservancy Committee under Schedule 7 to EPA 1990. This committee was not part of the Government's original plan for the NCC's reform but came about as an amendment to the legislation during its passage through Parliament. It does mean, however, that there is a body charged with viewing the interests of nature conservation as a whole in the United Kingdom and involved in international and European issues, rather than three separate bodies each having defined interests and possibly conflicting views.

**The Countryside Agency**

Formerly known as the Countryside Commission, this is a statutory body set up under section 47 of WCA 1981. Its administration is set out in Schedule 13 to WCA 1981. The Commission was renamed the Countryside Agency on 1 April 1999 following its merger with the Rural Development Commission. By means of the Development Commission (Transfer of Functions and Miscellaneous) Provisions Order 1999 the Commission was renamed and all references to it in any instrument or document before 1 April 1999 are deemed to have effect as if for that reference there were substituted "the Countryside Agency". Schedule 1 to the Order contains a list of all the amendments to primary legislation necessary in consequence of the name change and includes references to WCA 1981, NPACA 1949 and CA 1968.

Section 1 of NPACA 1949 sets out the functions of the Countryside Agency as:

> "(a)  the preservation and enhancement of natural beauty in England, both in national parks and areas of outstanding natural beauty .
> (b)  encouraging the provision and improvement, for persons resorting to national parks, of facilities for the enjoyment thereof and for the enjoyment of the opportunities for open air recreation and study of nature."

The Agency's main functions are designating of areas as national parks and as areas of oustanding natural beauty. Its general duties in relation to national parks are set out in section 6 of NPACA 1949. These include consideration generally, and in particular in relation to national parks, of what action is necessary to conserve and enhance the natural beauty, wildlife and cultural heritage of those areas. There is also a duty to keep under review the progress they make in accomplishing their purpose. The Agency is specifically charged with giving advice to the appropriate planning authority on administering an area as a national park and providing access for open-air recreation and facilities for the public visiting it.

## National parks authorities

National parks authorities (NPAs) are established by the Secretary of State by statutory instrument under powers now contained in the Environment Act 1995 (s 63). An NPA has a duty to carry out in relation to its national park the functions conferred by Part III of the 1995 Act. These include powers to do anything which, in the NPA's opinion, is calculated to facilitate or is conducive or incidental to:

(1) conserving and enhancing the park's natural beauty, wildlife and cultural heritage and of promoting opportunities for the understanding and enjoyment by the public of its special qualities; or
(2) carrying out functions conferred by any other enactment; and
(3) functions or duties set out in Schedules 8 and 9 to the 1995 Act.

**Local authorities**

Local authorities as local planning authorities (LPAs) have a vital function in relation to nature conservation. LPAs formulate policies for the preservation of nature conservation that will be adopted and implemented through their local plan. LPAs are at the sharp end of nature conservation and policies that are adopted in the local plan will be material considerations in any planning decision of the local authority.

Local authorities are bound to have regard to national and regional planning policy guidance and must give effect to statutory protections in place for the protection of habitats such as those contained in the Habitat Regulations 1994.

**Voluntary organisations and pressure groups**

There are other bodies with high profile reputations as guardians of the natural environment. These take the form of pressure groups, voluntary bodies or trusts for furthering nature conservation or local interest groups that have formed with the aim of protecting a particular species or conserving habitats or rare or endangered animals. Increasingly these groups have taken up the issue of conservation as it impinges on them. One of the oldest and best known is the Royal Society for the Protection of Birds (RSPB), established with the aim of reducing cruelty. Of the more modern national conservation groups Greenpeace and Friends of the Earth are probably the most high profile. A list of some of the more prominent organisations appears in Appendix A. Pressure groups have in the last two decades increasingly chosen to take their fight to save the natural environment to the courts. The RSPB were the appellants in the only UK case to challenge the implementation of the Birds Directive in the United Kingdom (*R* v *Secretary of State for the Environment, ex parte RSPB* - see p 18 below). The case was referred to the European Court of Justice (ECJ), and represents an important landmark in the willingness of pressure groups to challenge decisions of public authorities. This tendency to use the courts to attempt to enforce a particular interpretation of legislation is something that will increase in future. The willingness and the ability of these powerful interest groups to mount a legal challenge to unwelcome decisions should not be underestimated. Certainly their place as valid and powerful nature conservation bodies is established.

## *1.5* **Legislative framework**

### National Parks and Access to the Countryside Act 1949

The first significant piece of UK conservation legislation was the NPACA 1949. This legislation still governs the national park regime and is also the statute for the designation of nature reserves (s 15). The Act defines NNRs as areas managed for study or research into flora, fauna or of geological or physiographical interest or for preserving such features which are of special interest. NNRs must be areas under the complete control of English Nature - a prerequisite to any area being designated an NNR. The "control of the site" must be either freehold ownership, a lease of the land or a legally binding enforceable nature reserve agreement with the owner under section 16 of the Act. Any agreement concluded will be enforceable against successors in title to the land. Establishing an NNR involves English Nature in the expenditure of what may be considerable sums of money, either in acquiring ownership or leasing the land or paying compensation under the terms of a management agreement. Compensation is paid to the landowner for the withdrawal of his or her ordinary rights to use the land. In some cases operations that could be carried out on the land could be extremely lucrative, such as quarrying or peat cutting. Compulsory purchase is available to English Nature if it is unable to conclude a satisfactory nature reserve agreement under section 17 of NPACA 1949. This is also available where there is a breach of a nature reserve agreement. Any compulsory purchase order must be confirmed by the Secretary of State.

All NNRs are also designated SSSIs under WCA 1981 and there are no additional statutory restrictions in an NNR over and above those available to English Nature under the 1981 Act. There is an additional administrative power to make bylaws under section 20 of NPACA 1949.

The NPACA 1949 allows local authorities to designate and manage local nature reserves. Under section 21, LPAs are given power to designate sites of local importance. Before doing so subsection (6) obliges the LPA to consult with English Nature. LPAs' powers are the same as are available to English Nature to designate and manage reserves of national importance. In accordance with section 54A of the Town and Country Planning Act (TCPA) 1990, local authorities are obliged to have regard to the policies of the local development plan and must make decisions in accordance with it unless material considerations indicate otherwise.

A further nature conservation designation for areas of oustanding natural beauty (AONB) appears in the NPACA 1949. This designation relies chiefly on local authority protections through the planning system. A detailed consideration of AONB designation and the protection that it affords appears at p 69.

## Countryside Act 1968

This Act (CA 1968) gives English Nature the power to enter into management agreements with owners or occupiers of SSSIs (s 15). At the time CA 1968 was implemented to allow the negotiation of such agreements it was rarely utilised. It was not until WCA 1981 came into force that management agreements have been used on a far wider scale; their significance is considered in detail in Chapter 4. In carrying out its functions under the Act, English Nature is required to have regard to the needs of agriculture and forestry and the economic and social interests of rural areas. This act also confers power on a local authority to provide facilities for the public on common land and to make bylaws in respect of that land.

## Wildlife and Countryside Act 1981

This Act (WCA 1981) has for many years been the major governing legislation for designation of SSSIs and related conservation protections. It has been amended and updated by the Wildlife and Countryside Amendment Act 1985 and the Wildlife and Countryside Amendment Act 1991. It details the administrative requirements for designation of SSSIs and the duties on owners and occupiers in land so designated. The WCA 1981 extends to allow the establishment of marine nature reserves under section 36. It also provides for the more robust designation of a nature conservation order (NCO) and provides for offences for breach of both an SSSI designation and an NCO. The WCA 1981 also deals with species protection, although this has been strengthened and extended since the incorporation into UK law of the Habitats Directive by the Conservation (Natural Habitats, etc) Regulations 1994. A more detailed consideration of the WCA 1981 appears in Chapter 4 in relation to SSSIs and in Chapter 6 in relation to species protection.

**Environmental Protection Act 1990**

Although this Act was chiefly concerned with environmental protection measures rather than nature conservation, it implemented the reorganisation of the NCC into the three geographical Councils (see p 5 above). It also extended existing legislation in other respects, in particular the power of English Nature to conclude management agreements on land neighbouring SSSIs and NCO sites.

**Conservation (Natural Habitats, etc) Regulations 1994**

These Regulations graft onto the UK nature conservation and planning legislation protection for European sites designated under the Habitats Directive (see Chap 2). By means of these Regulations, certain internationally important sites already designated as SSSIs will be afforded additional protection if they are listed as SACs or SPAs. The effect of these Regulations is considered in detail in Chapter 3.

## *1.6* **Proposals for legislative change**

### SSSIs

The Department of the Environment, Transport and the Regions (DETR) in September 1998 issued a consultation document entitled *Sites of Special Scientific Interest: Better Protection and Management*, which proposes legislative change and other administrative measures within the existing SSSI framework to better protect and manage SSSIs. Proposals that may result in legislative changes include powers to simplify procedures for making boundary amendments to existing SSSIs and to allow the denotification of sites where the special interest in them has been lost. There are also proposals to amend legislation to increase penalties for deliberate damage to SSSIs and to enable restoration orders to be imposed in all cases. An intention is expressed in the document to introduce legislative amendment to provide English Nature with a power to refuse consent for damaging operations and a general right of access for English Nature to designated land or to assess a site for designation. The document states that the Government proposes to set up a working party to consider the options for marine sites and species.

The consultation document specifically proposes that the Government take action to ensure offences of damaging SSSIs are regarded with appropriate seriousness and concern and invites views on addressing the problem of third party damage. It also states that a more robust approach to taking enforcement action will be encouraged against those who deliberately damage special sites.

Replacement of Circular 4/83 (the financial guidelines for management agreements) is also proposed. It is intended to remove the presumption in respect of compensation in the form of net profit forgone. The document emphasises a shift in policy from payments to owners and occupiers to compensate for them refraining from a particular activity to payments relating to positive management agreements. These agreements will be individually targeted and offer payments for conserving and enhancing special interest.

Many of the proposals in the consultation document are a change to policy or administration intended to bring about improvements in the system of SSSIs, rather than amendment to the legislation itself. Examples are that English Nature will be requested to produce further advice for local authorites on protecting locally important sites from damage, and mechanisms for building on and improving informal liaison with owners and occupiers and for making information available to the general public. The Government will revise planning policy guidance to clarify and reinforce the appropriate degree of protection for SSSIs.

Other proposals to strengthen the system are the increased use of Site Objective and Site Management Statements for all SSSIs and requirements for owners on a sale of SSSI land to inform the new owner of the SSSI designation and to notify English Nature of the change in ownership.

## Access to the countryside

*Access to the Countryside: The Government's Framework for Action* was published in March 1999. It proposes a new statutory right of access to open countryside. The document sets out the Government's reasons for action, said to be necessary to redress the situation that has arisen over the period when the voluntary approach has been employed. The voluntary approach, in the

Government's view, "has delivered relatively little". The Government has promised a new statutory right which it believes will deliver the extent and permanence of access required.

The proposals are that a new statutory right of access on foot for open-air recreation will be created to specified categories of open countryside. The rights will apply to mountain, moor, heath and down and will be land shown on a map to be produced by the Countryside Agency. It will also extend to registered common land. Compensation will not be paid for general rights to access being required, although there are proposals for local authorities to assist with management of the new rights. The rights will be limited by the proposed legislation, however, and will not extend to agricultural land other than that extensively used for grazing. Presumably there will be definitions of the land to which the right applies contained within the legislation.

Restrictions are also proposed to enable landowners to close land or restrict access for a limited period, likely to be 28 days, in any one-year period. The reason for this must be for land management and notice of the proposed closure will be required to the appropriate authority. There will also be powers to close land for purposes of nature conservation and heritage, sound land management, health and safety and defence.

Local access forums will be established under the new proposals comprising representatives of interested groups. They will advise on issues of local relevance. A National Access Forum will complement the local groups discussing and advising on broader topics relating to the right of access, such as the proposed codes of practice for walkers and landowners.

Implementation of the proposals depends on the Government finding parliamentary time to introduce the new legislation required. The detail of the proposals will become clearer once a Bill has been introduced to implement them. It will be interesting to see how the legislation will tackle some of the problems envisaged, for example the definition of land to which access should apply. There may be other problems, which will become apparent on the implementation of the legislation, such as a landowner taking action to avoid land being classed as open country to the detriment of land of conservation value (*e.g.* by ploughing the site).

*Chapter 2*

# · Influences from Europe ·

## *2.1* Importance of European law and international influences

European Directives have had a major influence on conservation law in the UK over the past two decades. The influence of Europe and its role as a catalyst for change in UK legislation have resulted in a strengthening of nature conservation protections. This chapter considers the effects of the most significant Directives for nature conservation law and how they have been incorporated into UK legislation.

There have also been some influential international legal developments and international environmental law is one of the fastest growing influences on nature conservation law. International law is beyond the scope of this book, but international agreements such as the Convention on Wetlands of International Importance Especially as Waterfowl Habitats (known as the 1971 Ramsar Convention) have been of sufficient significance to influence European directives in their approach. The Ramsar Convention, for example, was the first global agreement to concern itself with a particular type of habitat aiming to protect and enhance wetlands. Parties to the Convention are under an obligation to formulate and implement wetland conservation and the deletion of listed wetlands is permitted only on grounds of "urgent national interest". A similar formula is employed in the Habitats Directive. The important influence of global Conventions should not be underestimated in influencing conservation law thinking, and the holistic approaches of the more recent Conventions on, for example, biodiversity are leading the way in approaches to conservation issues.

## *2.2* The Birds Directive

The Council Directive on the Conservation of Wild Birds (79/409/EEC) ("the Birds Directive") was one of the first European Community measures concerning nature protection. From an initial resolution in

1975 urging the Commission and the Council to "propose and adopt in the near future practical measures for the protection of migratory birds", the Directive was not finally adopted until some four years later.

The Birds Directive contains two distinct sets of provisions. In Articles 3 and 4 it addresses the protection of habitats of wild birds, and in Articles 5-9 the protection of particular wild bird species. The Directive therefore requires Member States to take measures, which include the creation of protected areas, to maintain a sufficient diversity of habitats for all European bird species, and to take special conservation measures in relation to particularly rare species of bird. The rare bird species are listed in Annex I to the Directive. Under the Directive Member States designate special protection areas (SPAs) for such birds.

## Designation of SPAs

Article 1 of the Birds Directive states that it applies to "all species of naturally occurring birds in the wild state in the European territory of the Member State to which the Treaty applies". The obligation on Member States in relation to those species of naturally occurring birds is, under Article 2, to "take the requisite measures to maintain the population of the species at a level which corresponds in particular to ecological, scientific and cultural requirements, while taking account of economic or recreational requirements, or to adapt the population of these species to that level". Article 3 requires Member States to "take the requisite measures to preserve, maintain or re-establish a sufficient diversity and area of habitats for all the species of birds" to which the Directive applies. Article 4(1) states that the species under Article 1 "shall be the subject of special conservation measures concerning their habitat" and that "Member States shall classify in particular the most suitable territories in number and size as special protection areas for the conservation of these species". Article 4(4) provides that Member States' obligations extend to avoiding pollution and deterioration of habitats.

The obligation imposed by the Birds Directive is, then, to designate under it SPAs for the protection of wild birds. The question of how much discretion is available to a Member State in carrying out that designation is one that has been considered by the European Court of Justice (ECJ). From its judgment in *Commission* v *Spain* (Case C-355/90), more commonly known as the *Santona Marshes* case, the conclusion can be drawn that any such discretion is limited. The court referred to the objective ornithological criteria contained in Article 4, which if satisfied in a particular case obliged the Member State concerned to designate an SPA. What is also evident from the judgment is that if an area constitutes one of the most important habitats for a number of endangered species of bird, this is sufficient for the criteria to be satisfied.

## Implications of Santona Marshes

The *Santona Marshes* case concerned Spain's failure to classify an area of coastal marshland, the Marismas de Santona, as an SPA. It is an important case, not only because it offers guidance on the interpretation of the Birds Directive, but also because it establishes that Member States cannot avoid or delay the classification of SPAs. The Santona Marshes is home to the spoonbill, a bird listed in Annex I to the Directive, and other migratory species visited the area, which raised a prima facie case for the area to be designated as an SPA under Article 4. The Commission had received complaints about a number of activities in the Santona Marshes. These included the creation of industrial zones and the inappropriate reclamation of land (including wetlands) in the region, the construction of a new road, the storage and disposal of untreated waste water in the area and the inappropriate grant of permits to carry out clam breeding in the area. Spain had failed to designate the area of the Marismas de Santona as an SPA under the Birds Directive and the court found that its failure to designate was a breach of its obligations under Articles 1 and 2. It also found that Spain had not taken the appropriate measures to prevent the deterioration of the habitats in the area contrary to the Article 4 provisions. The court specifically stated that it would not be possible to achieve the Directive's objectives if Member States' obligations under Article 4(4) to avoid pollution or deterioration of habitats or any disturbances affecting the birds only arose once designation as an SPA had occurred.

The judgment's practical implications are that Member States cannot avoid their obligations by delaying or avoiding the classification of SPAs. This means that there is an additional weapon in the armoury of interest groups involved in bird protection as the applicability of Article 4(4) is not in any way conditional upon the prior classification as an SPA and has direct effect on Member States. Prior to the judgment, academic opinion seemed to be that Article 4(4), because of its references to Article 4(1) and (2), which give Member States considerable discretion, could not be of direct effect. The exact form the measures should take, once the ornithological criteria determined by the Birds Directive are met - especially in terms of size and extent of any SPA - are still matters of considerable discretion simply because the Directive itself makes no provision.

### The UK experience

Judgment has been handed down in the first national case to test the Birds Directive in *R* v *Secretary of State for the Environment*, *ex parte RSPB* (case C-44/95)[1997] QB 206. The RSPB challenged the UK Government's decision to exclude an area of inter-tidal mudflat known as Lappel Bank from the Medway Estuary SPA. Lappel Bank immediately adjoined the Port of Sheerness, and the whole area has important ornithological qualities and is used by a number of wildfowl and water species. The area was described as "an important component of the overall estuarine ecosystem" and the loss of it, it was anticipated, would result in a reduction of the wader and wildfowl populations of the Medway Estuary.

The company operating the Port of Sheerness wanted to expand its operations and the physical expansion necessary for this could only be achieved by reclamation and development of Lappel Bank. The port itself is the fifth largest in the United Kingdom for freight and cargo and had particular natural features that made it able to accommodate both small and deep-sea vessels. As one of the few ports in the South East of England offering such facilities, it had developed into a thriving commercial enterprise. It was also a significant employer in the area, which had at the time a serious unemployment problem. The chance to extend the port, it was argued, would enable the Port of Sheerness to compete more effectively with large continental ports.

The Secretary of State took the view that the need not to inhibit the port's viability and the significant contribution that expansion into the area of Lappel Bank would make to the local and national economy outweighed the Bank's nature conservation value. The Secretary of State as a consequence of this excluded Lappel Bank from the designated area of the Medway SPA to allow the proposed expansion to go ahead. He did stress, however, that his decision was "an exceptional one taken to ensure the economic future of Sheerness and the Isle of Sheppey".

The RSPB challenged the Secretary of State's decision to exclude Lappel Bank from the SPA. The arguments in the case centred on whether it was acceptable to take into account economic factors in the decision-making process in designation of an SPA and the extent of the SPA. The Secretary of State argued that economic factors were relevant, but the RSPB relied on the ECJ's decision in *Santona Marshes* to support its argument that at the designation stage ornithological criteria only were relevant in the decision-making process. In the Court of Appeal the majority of the judges found for the Government; the RSPB appealed that decision and the House of Lords referred the case for consideration by the ECJ.

In its judgment the ECJ held that a Member State was not authorised to take account of the economic requirements mentioned in Article 2 of the Birds Directive when designating an SPA and defining its boundaries. Applying the precedent of *Santona Marshes*, the court ruled that it was clear from that case that economic requirements cannot on any view correspond to a general interest superior to that represented by the Birds Directive's ecological objectives. The court here went on to consider the amendment introduced to the Birds Directive by means of the Habitats Directive (considered further at p 23 below) and held that the Birds Directive is to be interpreted as meaning that a Member State may not, when designating an SPA and defining its boundaries, take account of economic requirements which may constitute imperative reasons of overriding public interest of the kind referred to in Article 6(4) of the Habitats Directive.

In the *RSPB* case the practical effects of the ECJ judgment have not been felt. The proposed development already had the benefit of planning permission and the House of Lords, although pressed to grant an injunction preventing development from going ahead, was not prepared to grant one. If this course had been followed then the decision to refer the case to the ECJ may have saved this part of the SPA by ensuring that the findings of that court would have to be adhered to. Unfortunately by the time the court gave judgment the project to extend the port had been completed and the Lappel Bank area destroyed. However, the importance of the decision should not be underestimated: a strict rule has now been established which cannot be overridden by administrative preference for economic considerations over the interests of conservation. The result of the decision is that where a site is identified as a potential SPA by meeting the ornithological criteria laid down in the Birds Directive, then economic considerations cannot now be used as to justify a failure to designate it. The economic potential of an area for a use  is at designation stage an irrelevant consideration.

### Reductions or modifications to an SPA

ECJ case law has also considered the extent to which Member States can reduce or modify an SPA. This has proved to be a contentious issue and one that resulted in an amendment to the Birds Directive by the Habitats Directive (considered below) to give more flexibility to Member States following the ruling in *Commission* v *Germany* (C57/89) (the *Leybucht Dykes* case). In this case (in which the UK Government supported the German authorities) it was proposed to carry out the reinforcement of a dyke in the Leybucht area of northern Germany. The area in question was already designated an SPA under the Birds Directive. The reinforcement of the dyke was considered necessary to protect human life, the existing dyke being liable to breach by water. However, in undertaking the works the German Government decided to change the line of the dyke to the benefit of the Leybucht harbour. This would result in a reduction in the SPA's size and significance. The court here found that the danger of floods and protection of the coastline were sufficiently genuine reasons to justify the dyke improvement works, but that those works should be kept to a strict minimum and involve only the smallest possible reduction in the SPA.

The question for the court in this case was to establish whether and if so under what conditions Member States were entitled to reduce the SPA's size and under what circumstances other interests may be taken into account. In considering the provisions of Article 4(4) of the Birds Directive the court held that, although Member States enjoyed a certain margin of discretion in selecting the most appropriate territories to be classified as SPAs under Article 4(1), they cannot exercise a similar margin of discretion under Article 4(4) in altering or reducing the size of such areas. This is because they themselves had acknowledged in their declarations that those areas offer the most appropriate living conditions for the species listed in Annex I. If this were not the case Member States could unilaterally evade their obligations under Article 4(4). The court held that any reduction in an SPA's size could only be justified on exceptional grounds. These grounds must amount to a public interest which is superior to the general interest represented by the Directive's ecological objective. The court held that in considering what is an interest superior to the general interest, the interests listed in Article 2 of the Directive, namely economic and recreational interests, could not be taken into account.

The court in *Leybucht Dykes*, in interpreting the Directive to require more extensive protection of SPAs than is provided for by legislation in many of the Member States, strengthened EC nature conservation legislation and the EC's influence on land use planning. The judgment set a strong precedent in ensuring that an SPA designation could not be set aside simply where it was convenient or commercially advantageous to do so. However, the court's ruling also fuelled political pressures to amend the Birds Directive and this was effected by means of the Habitats Directive (see below). In the light of the fact that the ruling left considerable uncertainty over the precise degree of protection required, the Habitats Directive amendment may bring more certainty, although no case law is yet available on the interpretation of that Directive. For the time being the Habitats Directive has weakened the EC nature conservation regime, to the dismay of conservationists, by permitting considerations of a social and economic nature to be taken into account in the decision-making process. This is the position in English law now that the Directive is incorporated into UK legislation by means of the Conservation (Natural Habitats, etc) Regulations 1994.

## *2.3* **The Habitats Directive**

This Directive (92/43/EEC) is known and referred to as "The Habitats Directive". Although it makes some provision for the protection of wild flora and fauna, its prime importance is in the provisions it makes for habitat protection. This Directive seeks to establish a coherent network of sites to be known as Natura 2000, consisting of SPAs designated under the Birds Directive together with sites designated under the Habitats Directive known as Special Areas of Conservation (SACs). Both designations are referred to as "sites of Community importance". SACs under the Habitats Directive must be sites hosting a habitat type or a species listed in the annexes to the Directive. In addition, natural habitat types in danger of disappearance and species that are endangered are marked in the annexes with an asterisk and are labelled "priority natural habitat types" and "priority species", as defined by the Directive. "Priority natural habitat type" is defined as being of Community importance if it is danger of disappearance within its natural range, or has a small natural range, or represents an outstanding example of one or more of five biogeographical regions (Alpine, Atlantic, Continental, Macronesian and Mediterranean). "Priority species" is defined as endangered, vulnerable, rare or endemic and requiring particular attention.

**Obligations under the Directive**

Under the Habitats Directive the UK Government was obliged to send a list of proposed sites to the Commission which in turn will draw up a draft list of sites of Community importance from sites submitted by Member States. The UK Government set a target date of 5 June 1995 for submission of its list of sites. At the time of writing over 200 UK sites have been put forward, and this is still being added to; however, the Commission had not produced an adopted list of sites, which is expected in 2000. The list of sites proposed by each Member State is prepared having regard to the criteria set out in Annex III of the Directive. The Directive takes account of the fact that certain Member States may host a higher proportion of habitats worthy of protection. Thus, under Article 4, Member States whose sites hosting one or more priority natural habitat types and priority species represent more than 5% of their national territory may, in agreement with the Commission, request that the Annex 3 criteria be applied more flexibly in selecting all the sites of Community importance in their territory. This provision eases the rigours of the Directive where a country has a particularly high proportion of habitats worthy of protection relative to other Member States.

Once a site of Community importance has been adopted by the Commission, an obligation arises for a Member State to designate that site as a special area of conservation as soon as possible. The Habitats Directive gives Member States up to six years in which to carry out the designation. Although it appears a generous length of time in which to carry out the Directive's requirements it does mean that an important positive step is imposed by it. This is coupled with a procedure under Article 5 of the Directive for the Commission to unilaterally invoke its procedures in circumstances where it has concerns about the scientific data on which a Member State bases its selection of sites. Article 5 states that in exceptional circumstances where the Commission finds that a provisional list submitted by a Member State in accordance with its obligations under Article 4(1) fails to mention a site hosting a priority natural habitat type or priority species, a bilateral consultation procedure shall be initiated. This will occur where on the basis of relevant and reliable scientific information it considers action to be essential for the maintenance of that priority natural habitat type or for the survival of that priority species. The bilateral consultation procedure compares the Commission's scientific data with the Member State's data. Any such consultation period is effective for six months; if on the expiry of that period the dispute remains unresolved, the Commission will forward to the Council a proposal relating to the selection of the site as one of Community importance. The Council must then take a decision relating to the site within a period of three months of the Commission forwarding its proposal.

### Obligations arising from designation as SAC

Article 6 of the Habitats Directive sets out the obligations of Member States where a site has been designated an SAC. It imposes an obligation on Member States to establish the necessary conservation measures involving, if need be, appropriate management plans specifically designed for the sites or integrated into other development plans, and appropriate statutory, administrative or contractual measures which correspond to the ecological requirements of the habitat or species in question. The manner in which the UK Government implements these requirements is considered below. Article 6 also imposes an obligation for Member States to take appropriate steps to avoid, in SACs, the deterioration of natural habitats and the habitats of species, as well as disturbance of species for which the area has been designated. What is more, Article 6 provides that any project or plan not directly connected with or necessary to the management of the site but likely to have a significant effect on it, either individually or in combination with other plans or projects, shall be subject to appropriate assessment of its implications for the site in view of the site's conservation objectives. The authorities are only at liberty to agree to any project or plan having ascertained that it will not adversely affect the site's integrity.

As mentioned at pages 19 and 21 above when considering the Birds Directive, the Habitats Directive was amended in the light of the ECJ's robust decisions on a Member State's ability to amend or reduce the size of an SPA. The amendment resulted in Article 6(4) of the Habitats Directive, which provides that if, in spite of a negative assessment of the implications for the site and in the absence of alternative solutions, a plan or project must nevertheless be carried out for imperative reasons of overriding interest, including those of a social or economic nature, the Member State shall take all compensatory measures necessary to ensure that the overall coherence of Natura 2000 is protected. It shall inform the Commission of the compensatory measures adopted. Article 6(4) goes on to state that where the site hosts a priority natural habitat type and/or a priority species, the only considerations which may be raised are those relating to human health or public safety, or what the Directive calls "beneficial consequences" of primary importance for the environment. The only other situation is where, further to an opinion of the Commission, there are other imperative reasons of public importance.

It is important to understand in practical terms what the Directive means before considering its incorporation into English law. It does increase the protection available to designated SPAs or SACs as it has been incorporated into the UK nature conservation regime through the Conservation (Natural Habitats, etc) Regulations 1994 (see Chap 3) and consequently adds another "layer" of protection to certain sites. Even if it had not been implemented in this way, the Directive itself may in any event be directly enforceable against public bodies. Directives sufficiently precise about the ends to be achieved have been held by the ECJ to be directly effective against bodies that are an emanation of the state. Generally, the English courts have been willing to construe UK legislation to comply with EC law if it is passed in order to give effect to an EC Directive. The Regulations incorporated into English law largely repeat the Directive's wording and for this reason EC law on, for example, the interpretation of the Birds Directive is of relevance when questions arise, as they undoubtedly will, on the interpretation of the UK Regulations. It can be predicted confidently that doubts will occur on the interpretation of the Regulations because of the approach of the Government in incorporating the Directive almost word for word. The wording of a Directive is usually less precise than is expected for UK legislation. Its incorporation will undoubtedly gives rise to issues on its interpretation in the future. In any event, the Regulations are interpreted in accordance with the Directive.

**Key points**

The following guide to the Habitats Directive assists in simplifying the procedures it applies to Member States.

*Adoption of sites*

- Member States are obliged to identify sites in accordance with the criteria laid down in the annexes to the Directive. In the United Kingdom these sites will always be SSSIs and the existing UK provisions governing these sites will apply.

- The UK Government is obliged to send a list of sites to the Commission for the purpose of compiling its own list of sites of Community importance. A list of sites is already in existence and this appears as Appendix A to PPG9. Adoption by the Commission has not occurred at the time of writing. There are obligations to keep the list under review and to periodically inform the Commission of any updates to it.
- The Commission prepares a list of sites of Community importance which will contain sites of Member States that are:
    - SPAs under the Birds Directive;
    - SACs;
    - sites hosting a priority natural habitat type as defined in the Annex to the Directive; and
    - sites hosting priority species as defined in the Annex to the Directive.
- There will be allowances for Member States having a high proportion of habitat types or species.

*Action required by Member States*

- A Member State is obliged to designate a site on the Commission's list of Sites of Community importance as an SAC as soon as possible, but within six years at most.
- In a case where the Commission finds that a Member States list fails to mention a site hosting a priority natural habitat type or priority species, it may initiate a bilateral consultation procedure for comparing the scientific data used by each. During the consultation period the site will have the protection afforded under the Directive.
- Member States are under an obligation to encourage the management of features of the landscape of major importance for wild flora and fauna by means of their land-use planning and development policies.

*What designation means for protected land*

- Member States are obliged to establish the necessary measures of conservation. These are outlined in the Directive to include appropriate management plans specifically designed for the sites or integrated into other development plans, and appropriate statutory, administrative or contractual measures.

- Appropriate steps must be taken to avoid, in SACs, the deterioration of natural habitats and the habitats of species as well as disturbance of species for which the area has been designated.

- Any plan or project not directly connected with the management of the site but likely to have a significant effect on it either individually or in conjunction with other plans and projects shall be subject to appropriate assessment of its implications for the site in view of its conservation objectives.

- Agreement to any plan or project can only be given if it has been ascertained that the plan or project will not adversely affect the site's integrity.

- If appropriate, in making any decision on the effect of a plan or project the Member State should "obtain the opinion of the general public". This appears to require consultation at the least and in some cases a public inquiry.

- If there is a negative assessment of the implications and no alternative solutions exist a Member State may be able to carry out a plan or project where there are imperative reasons of overriding public interest. These may include reasons of a social or economic nature.

- If the site in question is one hosting a priority natural habitat type or a priority species, it attracts stronger protection. The only considerations which may be raised in this situation are those relating to human health or safety, consequences of primary importance for the environment or other reasons of overriding public interest.

# Chapter 3

# The Conservation · (Natural Habitats, etc) · Regulations 1994

## *3.1* Outline of the Regulations

The Regulations incorporate the Habitats Directive into UK law. They have the effect of grafting the additional protection measures contained in the Directive onto the existing SSSI and planning system. All sites designated under the Regulations are already designated as SSSIs. What is also important is that it is stated Government policy, as set out in PPG9, that all candidate sites for SAC designation and all sites on the list of Community importance should be treated in the same way as a designated site. In other words, all sites which have been put forward for designation under the Directive are treated as if the UK Government had already fulfilled its obligation under the Directive to designate sites as SACs within six years.

### Selection of sites

The Regulations in Part II make provision for the conservation of natural habitats and habitats of species. Regulation 7 deals with the selection of sites eligible for identification as of Community importance. It provides for the Secretary of State to propose a list of sites indicating which of those contain a natural habitat type listed in the Annex I to the Directive and which species native to the UK listed in the Annex II to the Directive the site hosts. The Regulations provide that the Secretary of State may modify the list as a result of carrying out the surveillance required by the Directive.

Under the Regulations the duty imposed on the Secretary of State to designate a site as an SAC is no greater than the duty imposed under the Directive, that is within six years of the inclusion of a site on the list. The Regulations, however, give the Secretary of State some leeway by allowing him or her to establish priorities for the designation of sites. This prioritisation is carried out in the light of:

(1) their importance for the maintenance and restoration at a favourable conservation status of the habitat type or species, and for the coherence of Natura 2000; and
(2) the threats of degradation or destruction to which those sites are exposed.


**European sites**

The term used in the Regulations to describe areas belonging to the Natura 2000 network is "European site". Regulation 10 defines "European site" as:

(1) an SAC;
(2) a site of Community importance, i.e. a site defined in the Habitats Directive as one that contributes significantly to the maintenance or restoration at a favourable conservation status of a habitat type or species listed in Annex I or II to the Habitats Directive;
(3) a site hosting a priority natural habitat type or priority species in respect of which the Commission has initiated consultation with the Government to compare scientific data; and
(4) an area classified under the Birds Directive as an SPA.

The Secretary of State is obliged under the Regulations to compile a register of European sites that he or she is also obliged to make available for public inspection at all reasonable hours, free of charge.


**Content of the Regulations**

The Regulations deal with various administrative requirements such as the Secretary of State notifying English Nature of entry on and amendment to the register under regulation 12. English Nature in turn must notify landowners and occupiers under regulation 13. The arrangements are similar to those employed under WCA 1981 and include a requirement to supply a copy of the relevant entry in the register. An entry in the register is also a local land charge just as it is where a site is designated an SSSI. The administrative arrangements also extend to management agreements. Regulation 16 provides that English Nature may enter into agreements with owners and occupiers of land forming part of or adjacent to a European site for the management, conservation, restoration or protection of the site, or any part of it. The regime is not an extension of English Nature's existing powers to enter into agreements under the NPACA 1949 and CA 1968. There are transitional arrangements in regulation 17 for the continuation in force of existing agreements entered into under the 1949 and 1968 Acts.

Of particular significance is the extension to the SSSI regime provided by regulation 18, which ensures that any notification of potentially damaging operations (PDOs) under the SSSI provisions in the WCA 1981 shall have effect for the Natural Habitats Regulations. Under regulation 18(2), English Nature may also amend the original notification to secure compliance with the Habitats Directive's requirements. By conferring this additional power on English Nature they are at liberty in the case of a European site to amend the PDOs contained in the original notification. This is extremely important in the battle to conserve sites as it enables English Nature to exercise flexibility in designating operations that should not be carried out at the site. In addition, English Nature can amend the notification of the flora, fauna or other features by virtue of which the site is considered to be of special interest.

For an amendment to be made the notice requirements will again apply, with English Nature obliged to give notice to owners and occupiers of a site. However, it does not require that in effect there is complete renotification of the site, as would any change to the designation under the WCA 1981.

The restriction on carrying out PDOs specified in the notification extends to land within a European site. Regulation 19 provides that a site owner or occupier shall not carry out or cause or permit to be carried out any operation specified in the notification unless:

(1) English Nature has been given notification of the proposal to carry out the operation and has given written consent to carry it out;
(2) the operation is carried out in accordance with the terms of a management agreement; and
(3) four months have expired from giving notice to English Nature that the operation is to be carried out.

Contravention of the regulation 19 provisions is a criminal offence liable to a fine not exceeding level 4 (£2,500) on the standard scale. The scale of fine is the same as for carrying out a PDO in an SSSI.

The court also has power under regulation 26 to impose, in addition to any other penalty, a restoration order requiring a convicted person to carry out, within a period of time specified in the order, operations for restoring the land. If an order is made by a court and is not complied with, the court may impose a fine for breach up to level five on the standard scale (£5,000). A defendant does have an opportunity to apply to the court for discharge of or amendment to the order where compliance with it has become "impractical or unnecessary" because of a change in circumstances. The onus is on the defendant to show that compliance is impractical or unnecessary in particular circumstances.

Regulation 20 requires English Nature in certain circumstances to make "an appropriate assessment of the implications for the site in view of the site's nature conservation objectives". This applies where application is made to carry out a PDO, and it forms part of a plan or project which is not connected with or necessary to the site's management and is likely to have significant effects on the site. This means that where there is a risk of some form of significant effect, an environmental assessment may be required before the application for consent can be considered. Preparation of a full environmental assessment should have regard to the Regulations governing an environmental assessment for planning projects which contain criteria by which the assessment is made. By regulation 20(2), consent can only be given by English Nature where it has ascertained that the plan or project will not adversely affect the site's integrity. If English Nature fails to give consent for the operation, but considers there is a risk that the operation may be carried out, it must notify the Secretary of State so that consideration can be given to his or her making a special nature conservation order (SNCO) in respect of the site.

## 3.2 Special nature conservation orders

The Secretary of State has power under the Regulations to make an SNCO. This is not the same device as a nature conservation order (NCO) under WCA 1981, as an SNCO gives the site considerably increased protection. The designation of an SNCO under regulation 22 allows a damaging activity to be prevented permanently.

**Procedures on making an SNCO**

The procedures for making an SNCO are contained in Schedule 1 to the Regulations. The Secretary of State can make the designation to cover any part of land under threat within a European site, so that it does not have to apply to the whole site. The procedures are similar to those for making of NCOs under WCA 1981 with requirements for publicity and local public inquiries in the case of opposed orders. An SNCO will take effect on its being made. There are provisions in the Regulations for orders to be amended or revoked, but any such amendment or revocation is subject to confirmation by the Secretary of State. Where any order is made it takes effect before any inquiry into it takes place. Notice is published that it has been made specifying a time for making objections to it and the manner in which they should be made. The Local Government Act 1972 provisions govern any inquiry held into an SNCO. If an order has already taken effect, the Secretary of State, after considering his or her inspector's report, may decide to take no action on the order, or to amend or revoke it as he or she thinks fit in the light of any representations or objections in the report. If the order is an amending or revoking order and requires confirmation, he or she may confirm it with or without modifications.

**PDOs in site subject to SNCO**

The Regulations provide for a permanent ban on carrying out PDOs in a European site the subject of an SNCO. A PDO may only be carried out if the owner or occupier has received English Nature's written consent to it or it is provided for in any management agreement that relates to the land. It cannot be carried out on expiry of a period of time, as is the case under the SSSI regime. A person who, without reasonable excuse, carries out any such operation is liable on summary conviction before the magistrates' court to a fine not exceeding the statutory maximum of £5,000. The offence is an either way offence and may be tried on indictment before the Crown Court. On conviction on indictment, the penalty of a fine is not subject to a maximum upper limit.

The Regulations themselves make some provision for what might be considered a "reasonable excuse" defence to a prosecution under regulation 23. Paragraph (3) provides that if the PDO was carried out in the case of an emergency, it may serve as a reasonable excuse. If this defence is to be employed the defendant must have provided particulars to English

Nature of the PDO and the nature of the emergency as soon as practicable after the PDO's commencement. Whether the emergency was sufficient and whether the notification of the nature of the emergency and the PDO carried out were undertaken promptly will be matters of fact and degree for consideration by the court in each case. It is also a reasonable excuse where the PDO was carried out in pursuance of a valid planning permission issued by the LPA. If this is the case, the procedures for notifying English Nature as a statutory consultee will have been undertaken prior to the issue of the permission.

**Consents for PDOs**

The circumstances where English Nature can give consent to a PDO in an SNCO site are restricted under the Regulations. Regulation 24 provides that where it appears to English Nature that an application for consent relates to an operation which forms part of a project or plan which is not directly connected with or necessary to the site's management, or is likely to have a significant effect on the site, English Nature must assess its implications for the site. The obligation on English Nature is to make this assessment, which could range from some form of environmental assessment to a written statement giving English Nature's opinion of the activity's effect, in view of the site's conservation objectives. Any assessment prepared in whatever form will not, therefore, take account of other factors such as the economic advantages to the owner or occupier of carrying out the PDO. The planning policy guidance note on nature conservation (PPG9) at Annex C deals with development control, and makes it clear that the scope and content of an appropriate assessment depends on the location, size and significance of the proposed project. In the light of the assessment's conclusions, English Nature may only give consent for the PDO having ascertained that the plan or project will not adversely affect the site's integrity. If consent is refused, English Nature is obliged to give reasons for the decision. There is an avenue of appeal against the refusal available to the site owner or occupier. Within two months of receiving notice of refusal of consent, or if no notice of a decision has been received within three months of an application for consent, the owner or occupier may require English Nature to refer the matter to the Secretary of State. It is necessary for the owner or occupier to give notice of this requirement to English Nature in writing.

The Secretary of State may give consent to the PDO if he or she is satisfied that the plan or project in question must be carried out for imperative reasons of overriding public interest. These may include reasons of a social or economic nature. If he or she is so satisfied, he or she may direct English Nature to give consent to the PDO.

### Consents where site hosts priority natural habitat type or priority species

If a site is one subject to an SNCO which hosts a priority natural habitat type or a priority species, the requirements for consent are even more restrictive. In such a case the only reasons to empower the Secretary of State to direct that consent should be given are those relating to human health, public safety or beneficial consequences of primary importance to the environment. As an alternative, consent may be given where there are other reasons which, in the European Commission's opinion, are imperative reasons of overriding public interest. If the Secretary of State should direct that consent is given under regulation 24, he or she is obliged to secure that such compensatory measures are taken to ensure the overall coherence of Natura 2000. It is interesting that the formula of reasons relating to human health or public safety - the test laid down by the ECJ in *Leybucht Dykes* (see p 20 above) - only applies if the site is a priority natural habitat site or hosts a priority species. This means that the test laid down by the ECJ in their interpretation of the Birds Directive has been weakened, as under the Habitats Directive that test will only apply to priority natural habitat sites or sites hosting a priority species. It would seem that showing "overriding public interest" where there is no threat to human health or public safety will be very difficult. The only other available route for the grant of consent is to apply to the Commission for an opinion of whether reasons are to be considered as imperative reasons of overriding public interest. Not to do so may leave the decision-maker open to challenge by an interested party. Challenges to decisions may be taken by interest groups or aggrieved individuals if the basis for the decision is open to question.

The requirements for consent to PDOs where they are likely to have a significant effect on an SNCO site are very strict. It is difficult to evaluate the practical effects of the Regulations, which are very much in their infancy. Major planning projects in any designated SNCO are less likely to secure the necessary consents to proceed, however, since the introduction of this improved conservation protection. It is unlikely that projects such as the extension to the Medway Estuary in the *RSPB* case (see p 18 above) will receive consents if they host a priority natural habitat type or priority species. This will be the case even having regard to the reasons of a social and economic nature put forward as justification for the *RSPB* decision.

Under regulation 25, where an SNCO is made English Nature is obliged to pay compensation to those who have an interest in the land if it is subject to agricultural use and can be shown to be of less value because the order has been made.

## *3.3* **The Regulations and planning controls**

Part IV of the Regulations deals with the adaptation of planning and other controls. All of the provisions apply to projects which would not usually require planning permission and are often Government backed, such as roads, pipelines and transport and works projects. They extend to IPC and LAAP controls (regs 48 and 49). These regulations require an LPA to consider the effects of granting a consent or planning permission on a European site. By regulations 83 and 84 they are applied to granting a local authority air pollution control authorisation under EPA 1990 or any waste management licence under that Act. By regulation 71 they are applied to consent granted under the Electricity Act 1989 and by regulation 75 to pipeline construction or diversion authorisation. By regulation 79 they are applied to transport and works authorisations under the Transport and Works Act 1992.

### Permitted development

The Regulations also remove in certain circumstances permitted development rights granted under the Town and Country Planning (General Permitted Development) Order 1995. The GPDO grants permission for activities and development listed in Schedule 2 to the Order so that those activities or development do not usually require planning permission. This has the effect of requiring a planning application to be submitted which can only be granted if English Nature is of the view that the operation will not adversely affect the site's integrity. In effect, in relation to GPDO powers, the Regulations qualify planning permission granted by the order and apply the regime laid down in the Regulations in its place.

Regulation 60 provides that:

> "It shall be a condition of any planning permission granted by a General Development Order whether made before or after the commencement of these Regulations that development which–
> (a)    is likely to have a significant effect on a European site, and
> (b)    is not directly connected with or necessary to the management of the site,
> shall not be begun until the developer has received written notification of the approval of the local planning authority."

It is surprising that regulation 60 encompasses permission granted by a general development order (GDO) made before the commencement of the Regulations in relation to a development that was begun but not completed before the commencement of the Regulations. The Regulations themselves provide that any such development shall not be continued until the developer has received written notification of the LPA's approval. Under regulation 61 it is open to an applicant to seek English Nature's opinion before carrying out development in reliance on permission granted by a GDO. In this way a developer can avoid application to the local planning authority directly, although English Nature is obliged to inform both the applicant and the LPA of its decision.

## Applicability of the Regulations

Any doubt over the applicability of the Regulations is catered for in regulations 61 and 62, which provide that where it is intended to carry out development in reliance on the permission granted by the GPDO, application may be made to the "appropriate nature conservation body" (English Nature) for its opinion of the development or the LPA for its permission. Regulation 61 provides that if English Nature is notified of the proposed development and is of the opinion that the development is not likely to have significant effects on a European site, this is conclusive proof of the project not having any such effect for the purposes of relying on the GPDO permission. The LPA may give permission for the activity proposed to be carried out under the GPDO, but only after taking account of any representations made by English Nature and making an appropriate assessment of the implications of the development for the site. For any landowner in a European site to rely on GPDO rights, he or she must first have ascertained from English Nature that in its opinion the proposals will not adversely effect the site.

If application is to be made to the LPA, the LPA is obliged under regulation 62(3) to assume for the purposes of considering the application that the development will have a significant effect on the site. This, coupled with the obligation to consult English Nature and to have regard to any representation it may make, means that from a practical point of view an application to English Nature may be by far the most administratively straightforward way of proceeding for a landowner.

**Applications for planning permission**

Under regulation 48, where application is made for planning permission or any other authorisation within the LPA's jurisdiction the LPA must consult English Nature and have regard to any representations made by it. The LPA as the "competent authority" under the Regulations must, before deciding to give any consent to a plan or project, make an appropriate assessment of the implications for the site in view of the site's nature conservation objectives. Part of the duty to make an appropriate assessment is to have regard to English Nature's representations. PPG9 states that "appropriate assessment" will depend on the location, size and significance of the proposed project. English Nature will advise on this on a case-by-case basis. At its simplest the requirement will be for a general statement of the development's impact; at the other extreme it could require a full environmental assessment.

Regulation 48 also rather curiously refers to the authority "taking the opinion of the general public if they consider it appropriate". Only having considered the conclusions of the assessment and having ascertained that the plan or project will not adversely affect the site's integrity can the authority grant the permission or consent sought. PPG9 offers the LPA some guidance on what is meant by "the integrity of the site". It states at Annex C: "the integrity of the site is the coherence of its ecological structure and function across its whole area that enables it to sustain the habitat, complex of habitats and levels of populations of the species for which it was classified". The grant of any consent or permission is subject to regulation 49, which provides that if the LPA is satisfied that the project must be carried out for imperative reasons of overriding public interest, it may agree to the plan or project notwithstanding a negative assessment of the implications for the site. Where the site hosts a priority natural habitat or priority species, the reasons constituting a reason of overriding public interest for granting consent must be either reasons relating to human health or public safety, beneficial consequences of primary importance to the environment, or other reasons which in the European Commission's opinion are imperative reasons. It seems that showing overriding public interest, where there is no threat to human health or public safety, effectively means applying to the Commission for an opinion on whether reasons are to be considered as imperative reasons of overriding public interest. Not to do so may leave the decision-makers open to challenge. The Regulations themselves make provision for a "competent authority", which includes an LPA, to request that the Secretary of State seek the Commission's opinion, although he or she is not bound to do so.

The Regulations are retrospective in certain respects. By regulation 50 they provide for review of existing decisions and consents where consent, permission or other authorisation has been given for a project to which regulation 48(1) would apply. That regulation requires an authority, before deciding to give permission or consent to a project or plan likely to have a significant effect on a European site, to make an appropriate assessment of the implications for the site in view of the site's conservation objectives. Regulation 50 provides that the authority in question shall as soon as reasonably practicable review its decision or the consent, permission or authorisation and affirm, modify or revoke it. This means that any decision made prior to the Regulations coming into force for authorising a project which is likely to have a significant effect on the site and is not directly connected with the management of it must be subject to review. This will apply where any extant planning permission is still within time for implementation or permission is implemented but not yet completed. Any developer proposing to implement such a permission should be aware of the duty to review the grant of that permission in the light of the Regulations and the new criteria they lay down for nature conservation. The considerations for the LPA on review, provided for in regulation 51, are those which the LPA would have had to consider were the review an application for any such decision or consent at first instance.

## Consent required from more than one authority

Regulation 52 is likely to apply in the case of major planning projects. It addresses the situation where a plan or project is undertaken by or consent is required from more than one "competent authority". A competent authority is defined by regulation 6 as including any LPA, public or statutory undertaker and government department. Where any plan or project requires the consent, permission or authorisation of more than one competent authority or is undertaken by one or more competent authorities, regulation 52 applies. This states that nothing in the Regulations should be taken as requiring a competent authority to assess any implications of a plan or project that would be more appropriately assessed by another competent authority. It provides for a clear division of responsibilities where, for example, both English Nature and a harbour authority have an interest in a site. The harbour authority is properly responsible for the conduct of vessels in the harbour, for instance, but has little or no expertise in assessing any proposals having regard to a site's nature conservation objectives. The wording of the Regulations imply that a harbour authority, for example, should not be burdened with considering nature conservation issues where the relevant nature conservation body is the more competent body or to consider planning issues where the planning authority is the more competent authority. There is potential for conflicts to arise here, but the assessment of the site in view of its nature conservation objectives seems to point to the nature conservation objectives taking priority over other interests. The Secretary of State has power under regulation 52(3) to issue guidance to authorities on the circumstances in which an authority may or should adopt the reasoning or conclusions of another competent authority. It is clearly important to refer to any guidance that may be issued.

Provision is made in the Regulations for special development orders, simplified planning zones, enterprise zones, construction or improvement of highways or roads and proposed orders under the Transport and Works Act 1992 to fall within the Regulations. There are also provisions relating to consent under the Electricity Act 1989 and the Pipelines Act 1962. Any practitioner dealing with applications for consents in an SNCO site should be aware of the applicability of the Regulations.

**Other powers contained in the Regulations**

The Regulations are extremely detailed. Certain miscellaneous provisions contained in the Regulations should also be mentioned.

Regulation 28 confers power on the Nature Conservancy Council to make bylaws for the protection of a European site.

Regulation 87 makes provision for agreement with the appropriate nature conservation body to circumvent the four-month restriction on carrying out operations specified in a notification of PDOs under regulation 18. (This will apply in a European site, but not in a site subject to an SNCO.)

Regulation 90, which provides for powers of entry, grants power to a person authorised in writing by the appropriate nature conservation body to enter any land to ascertain:

(1) whether an SNCO should be made in relation to that land, or if an offence under the Regulations has been committed; or
(2) the amount of compensation payable to any person entitled to it under the provisions of regulation 25.

There is some restriction on the power. It is necessary, where any land is occupied, for 24 hours' notice to be given to the occupier. The power does not extend to entry to any dwelling on the land. The notice requirement does not apply where the purpose of entry is to establish whether an offence has been committed.

Regulation 99 provides for powers of entry in relation to surveying land in connection with a claim for compensation or with the acquisition of any interest in it, whether by agreement or compulsory acquisition.

Regulation 107 enables the Secretary of State to cause a local inquiry to be held to exercise any of his or her functions under the Regulations.

## 3.4 **The importance of PPG9**

The Government planning policy guidance note on nature conservation provides comprehensive advice on the relationship between planning control and nature conservation. It is an important document because planning authorities are obliged to take account of it in preparing their development plans. The essential task of LPAs and all public agencies concerned with the use of land and natural resources, as described in the guidance, is to make adequate provision for development and economic growth whilst ensuring effective conservation of wildlife and natural features. The guidance describes environments where attention is given to nature conservation as "essential to social and economic well being". It firmly states that, with careful planning and control, conservation and development can be compatible.

PPG9 states that it is Government policy that any proposal affecting candidate SAC sites should be considered by the LPA as if that site were a designated SAC; a similar approach is taken to potential SPAs. This means that candidate sites attract the same legal protection as designated sites.

The PPG also states that LPAs should take nature conservation objectives into account in all planning activities that affect rural and coastal land use, and in urban areas where there is wildlife of local importance. It goes on to insist that they should be taken into account in regional planning guidance, structure plans, unitary development plans and local plans. The guidance stresses that nature conservation issues are not confined by administrative boundaries, and that species other than man do not recognise national boundaries, bringing home to LPAs and other land use planning bodies the need to take a holistic view of nature conservation.

PPG9 offers useful guidance to LPAs in tabular form on consideration of development proposals affecting SPAs and SACs and on the applicability of permitted development rights. These are reproduced at Appendices C and D. More detailed consideration of the guidance in PPG9 appears at p 116.

**Key points**

*Designation of sites*

- The Conservation (Natural Habitats, etc) Regulations incorporate the Habitats Directive into UK law by grafting the additional protection measures onto the existing SSSI and planning system.
- All sites designated under the Habitats Regulations and terrestrial Ramsar sites are already SSSIs.
- The Government has made it clear in PPG9 that all candidate sites for designation under the Habitats Regulations should be treated in the same way as a designated site.
- The Regulations use the term "European site" which encompasses SACs, sites on the list of Community importance held by the Commission, sites hosting a priority natural habitat type or priority species and SPAs under the Birds Directive.

*Potentially damaging operations*

- A PDO may only be carried out if English Nature has given written consent to it or it is carried out in accordance with the terms of a management agreement or four months have expired from the landowner giving notice of his or her intention to carry it out.
- Carrying out a PDO in breach of regulation 19 is a criminal offence liable to a fine not exceeding level 4 (£2,500).
- English Nature is required to make "an appropriate assessment of the implications of the site in view of the site's nature conservation objectives". These obligations apply where application is made to carry out a PDO which forms part of a plan or project not connected with or necessary to the site's management and likely to have significant effects on the site. Consent may only be granted by English Nature where it has ascertained that the plan or project will not adversely affect the site's integrity.
- SNCO designation allows a damaging activity to be prevented permanently.
- PDOs may only be carried out in an SNCO site with English Nature's written consent or where such activities are provided for in a management agreement. There is no provision for expiration of a time period.
- Any PDO carried out in breach of the SNCO is liable on summary conviction to a maximum £5,000 fine or an unlimited fine on indictment.
- Where an SNCO site hosts a priority natural habitat type or priority species requirements for consent are reasons relating to human health, public safety or beneficial consequences of primary importance to the environment.
- The LPA must, before deciding to give any consent, make an appropriate assessment of the implications for the site in view of the site's conservation objectives. The LPA is obliged to have regard to any representation made by English Nature.
- If the LPA is satisfied that the plan or project must be carried out for imperative reasons of overriding public interest, it may agree to the plan or project notwithstanding a negative assessment of the implications for the site.
- Where the site hosts a priority natural habitat type or priority species, the reason of imperative overriding public interest must

be reasons relating to human health or public safety or beneficial consequences of primary importance to the environment, or other reasons which in the Commission's opinion are imperative.
- The Regulations extend to consents under the Electricity Act 1989, the Pipelines Act 1962, the Transport and Works Act 1992, environmental controls and highway and road projects.
- There is a bylaw making power available. Whether bylaws exist should be checked in relation to a site.

## Powers of entry and PPG9

- Powers of entry are available to English Nature to establish whether an SNCO should be made in relation to any land or if an offence has been or is being committed on land which is a European site.
- By means of guidance in PPG9 the Government has stated its policy in relation to candidate SAC sites is that they should be dealt with as if designation had already occurred under the Regulations.

*Chapter 4*

# Sites of Special Scientific Interest

## 4.1 Designation of sites

### Selection of SSSIs

SSSIs are selected on scientific grounds. They are not (as are some other designations) selected for the purpose of advancing amenity or recreation. Sites are selected to be representative of habitats of special value and the rationale behind their selection is to provide, throughout the UK, sites representative of differing habitats and features. Sites designated are usually outstanding examples of their type.

English Nature, under the Wildlife and Countryside Act (WCA) 1981 has a positive duty to designate SSSIs. This specific duty is important in that no discretion exists at the designation stage. In challenging the designation of a site its owner or occupier has limited scope to object or negotiate terms to his advantage.

### Notification under WCA 1981 - procedure for designation

Under the procedures detailed in section 28 of and Schedule 11 to WCA 1981, English Nature is obliged to notify designation of a site to every owner or occupier, as well as the LPA, the Environment Agency and the Secretary of State. The notification specifies to the owner and occupier what feature of interest in or on the land means that it is of special interest. It also lists what operations appear likely to damage that flora or fauna of special interest. The notification contains notice of a three-month period for objections or representations to be made to English Nature concerning the designation.

Representations may take the form of requests to amend the proposed boundaries of the SSSI site or for the exclusion of certain activities from the list of potentially damaging operations, which tend to be drafted extremely broadly. Such representations should be in writing and the importance of careful drafting and, where possible, supporting evidence is emphasised. Evidence usually needs to challenge the scientific basis of the designation itself. Any representations must be considered by English Nature, which has a period of nine months from the date of notification in which to assess whether that notification should stand and to confirm, modify or discharge it. Where any representation is accepted, English Nature has the power to make the notification with modifications under section 28(4A) of WCA 1981.

The courts recently considered the notification of sites in *R v Nature Conservancy Council, ex parte London Brick Property Ltd* [1996] Env LR 1. Here, by reason of pumping operations connected with the extraction of clay at the site and the subsequent landfill that took place, a network of shallow saline pools was formed, an environment suitable for a rare species of water beetle. In February 1993 English Nature decided to notify the site as an SSSI under section 28. Pumping of the site, which had resulted in the creation of the unique environment suitable for the beetle, ceased before notification was carried out. The question for the court was whether English Nature had acted perversely in deciding to notify the site even though the action which caused it to be of special value had ceased. The court considered there were two steps to notification:

(1) A duty was imposed on English Nature under section 28(1) to notify a site that fulfils appropriate criteria. No discretion exists at this stage. This has a provisional effect and allows a three-month period for representations and objections.
(2) English Nature must consider any representations or objections and then has discretion under section 28(4A) to confirm the notification with or without modifications. If no confirmation occurs within nine months of the original notification, then the notification lapses.

The court here held that it was not unreasonable for English Nature to identify the site in the hope that London Brick would co-operate to retain it.

### Potentially damaging operations

When the original notification is issued and served on owners and occupiers it contains a list of operations which in English Nature's opinion would have an adverse affect on the integrity of the SSSI's value. This is commonly referred to as the "list of potentially damaging operations". It lists those activities prohibited until the landowner has given notice to English Nature of an intention to carry it out and been granted permission for it, or allowed the requisite time period of four months to elapse before carrying it out. A sample list of operations which might be noted as likely to damage the features of special interest appears at Appendix B.

## *4.2* **Effect of designation**

The list of potentially damaging operations (PDOs) constitutes the first restriction on landowners and occupiers in an SSSI. It does not have the effect of permanently restricting the carrying out of operations by itself, but it requires the landowner or occupier to adhere to certain procedures before carrying out any operation listed as potentially damaging.

If a landowner wishes to carry out an operation included in the list, he or she must first notify English Nature. The list of PDOs is usually widely drawn to include any number of operations which might ordinarily be carried out on land regularly (*e.g.* cutting vegetation or digging the soil), and it is advisable to be familiar with the entire contents of the list. A frequent problem for landowners is to carry out an activity which is a PDO on the land without realising that this is the case.

Once English Nature has been notified of an intention to carry out an operation by the owner or occupier, four possible consequences may flow:

(1) Permission to carry out the operation may be received and the owner or occupier can go ahead with it.
(2) No express permission is received, so that on expiry of the four-month period from giving the notice the owner or occupier may carry it out in any event.
(3) English Nature will open negotiations, within the four-month period, with the owner or occupier in an attempt to negotiate the terms of a management agreement for the site. This may trigger certain compensation payments to the owner or occupier in consideration of him or her giving up his or her rights to carry out certain operations or activities on the land. This may arise for land used for agriculture or forestry. An examination of management

agreements and the compensation payments they may give rise to are considered at pages 51-53 below.

(4) If no management agreement can be negotiated, English Nature may instigate procedures for the purchase of the land compulsorily or, if possible, negotiate its purchase with the landowner; this is a rare occurrence. As an alternative, imposition of a more restrictive nature conservation designation may be considered, such as an NCO, which will extend the period in which the owner cannot carry out PDOs.

## *4.3* **Planning permission and SSSIs**

Designation as an SSSI does not remove the need for planning permission for operations or activities that would in the normal course of events require such permission. Permission is required for the "development" of land, a concept defined in section 55 of TCPA 1990. Section 55(2) defines development as the carrying out of "building, engineering, mining or other operations in, on, or over land". Planning permission is also required on any change of use of the land (*e.g.* on changing part of a field into a garden for a residential property). On any application for planning permission in an SSSI the LPA is obliged to consult English Nature as a statutory consultee; if English Nature objects the LPA may request that the Secretary of State call in the application for determination.

If an application is called in by the Secretary of State, he or she will appoint an inspector to prepare a report after considering all the evidence at public inquiry. The inspector's report to the Secretary of State will contain a recommendation, but the decision is for the Secretary of State alone. Where planning permission is granted it overrides the SSSI designation and the landowner can carry out the authorised activity. In other words, a valid planning permission is a defence to a prosecution for carrying out PDOs on land in breach of an SSSI designation.

### Permitted development

Normal agricultural activities not usually requiring planning permission or rights exercised under the Town and Country Planning (General Permitted Development) Order 1995 are preserved for any landowner. However, the notification procedures to English Nature in respect of PDOs and requirement for permission (or the four-month time delay) still apply under the SSSI regime governing the land.

There are restrictions in excess of this where the land is designated an internationally important site under the Conservation (Natural Habitats, etc) Regulations 1994. Article 60 of the Regulations imposes a condition that development in an SPA or SAC shall not begin until the LPA's written notification of approval has been obtained. On consideration of the proposals, the LPA is obliged to supply English Nature with a copy of the application and to take account of any representations made by it.

There may also be sites where a direction under Article 4 of the General Permitted Development Order 1995 has been made by the LPA or the Secretary of State. Where such a direction has been given, the direction will specify any paragraph or class of the Order (except certain classes dealing with minerals, which are excluded from Article 4) for which development rights under the Order shall not apply. In such cases it is necessary for a planning application to be submitted.

## Considerations on planning application for land in an SSSI

Any representations made by English Nature to the LPA on a planning application constitute a material consideration. This is important: it means that English Nature's advice is a factor to be weighed in the balance by the LPA when making a planning decision. The representations do not, however, constitute an overriding consideration in any LPA decision. PPG9, issued by the then Department of the Environment in 1994, gives LPAs guidance on how to deal with nature conservation objectives in their land use and development control functions and contains guidance on the protection of individual protected species. The guidance stresses that the key importance of SSSIs means that development proposals in or likely to affect them must be subject to special scrutiny, and gives particular guidance on consultation with English Nature and, where special procedures apply, to protect sites of particular importance. Guidance in PPG9 advises LPAs that nature conservation objectives should be taken into account in all planning activities which affect rural and coastal land use, and in urban areas where there is wildlife of local importance. Nature conservation objectives should be reflected in regional planning guidance, structure plans, unitary development plans and local plans to comply with PPG9.

A further consequence of designation is the inclusion on the register of local land charges under section 28(11) of WCA 1981. Prospective purchasers of land are made aware, by this means, of the fact that the land is subject to an SSSI designation.

In some cases a consultation zone exists on land neighbouring an SSSI. English Nature may require consultation for an area around an SSSI under powers in the GPDO. Where such a zone has been notified to the LPA, it will notify English Nature of development proposals in that zone. The consultation zone is meant as a device to prevent activities on neighbouring land, such as drainage of wetlands affecting the SSSI site.

## *4.4* **Concept of potentially damaging operations**

### Notification of PDOs

In carrying out notification to owners and occupiers, English Nature will have included notification of what are considered PDOs. These PDOs relate to the features of the land which are of special interest. The operations are those likely to damage those features of special interest.

Section 28(7) of WCA 1981 provides that it is an offence, without reasonable excuse, for the owner or occupier to carry out or cause or permit to be carried out a PDO. This is the case unless the four-month period of notice has elapsed or English Nature has given consent to the operation. Breach of section 28(7) carries on summary conviction a penalty of a fine not exceeding level four on the standard scale (£2,500). The offence is one of strict liability. The offence of carrying out PDOs in breach of the designation applies only in relation to owners and occupiers, a recognised weakness of the regime. The consequences of this are that categories of persons who may cause damage to a site's integrity (*e.g.* trespassers) cannot be prosecuted for carrying out a PDO.

PDOs are usually wide ranging and the courts have not used the limited definition of "operations" contained in TCPA 1990. However, many PDOs do not in themselves constitute development for TCPA 1990 purposes.

### Scope of PDOs

The scope of PDOs were examined in *Sweet* v *Secretary of State for the*

*Environment* [1989] 2 PLR 14. The applicant owned three meadows and adjoining ditches within Westhay Moor in Somerset. An NCO was made under section 29 of WCA 1981; this is a stronger conservation designation offering greater protection for a site (see p 55). In respect of the PDOs listed in the schedule to the NCO, the applicant contended that there were specified a number of operations which, under the terms of section 29(3), could not be prohibited operations. This was because they were agricultural activities that would not result in some physical alteration to the land of some permanence. It was argued that the Act made a distinction between "activities" and "operations", and "operations" had a particular meaning in planning legislation that did not include agricultural activities. It was held, however, that although the word "operations" is used in WCA 1981, and is a term of art in planning legislation, such legislation is not of assistance in construing the Act. The court held that the purpose of the words used in the Act was wide enough to cover all the operations specified as PDOs in the NCO made in respect of the land.

## Meaning of "operation"

*Sweet* is an interesting case and has considerable practical ramifications because it establishes that an "operation" need not be an activity which results in some physical alteration to the land or which has some degree of physical permanence. An operation can be an ordinary agricultural activity or indeed an ordinary everyday activity, such as exercising a dog, if that activity is listed as a PDO in relation to the land. The extent of the PDOs is, then, a matter of particular importance for a landowner and it is one on which negotiation with English Nature might be of particular benefit.

Thus the initial practical restrictions on designation of land as an SSSI stem from the list of PDOs and effectively mean that there will be at least a four-month ban on carrying out any of those operations. This period runs from the time the landowner or occupier gives English Nature notice of an intention to carry them out. Giving notice, however, may have other consequences, including steps being taken to take control of the land. For this purpose, English Nature has powers available to it to negotiate a management agreement or, in extreme cases, to initiate compulsory acquisition of the land.

The importance of a landowner giving careful consideration to the extent of any designation is underlined by the fact that once the designation is complete, English Nature is not thereafter at liberty to change the list of PDOs. Any proposed change to the list requires English Nature to redesignate the site with a revised list of PDOs. The importance of careful examination of the proposed list of PDOs is significant in attempting to minimise the effects of the designation for the landowner.

## *4.5* **Management agreements and compensation**

### Circumstances in which compensation may be payable

The period of four months' grace permitted to English Nature under the legislation has a significant practical purpose. It is designed to allow English Nature to assess the likely impact of the proposed PDO on the site and, if the activity is judged to have an adverse effect, to attempt to negotiate a management agreement safeguarding the nature conservation interest. If no agreement is successfully concluded within the four-month period, the landowner may proceed with the activity. In this respect the regime concerning the protection of SSSIs is a voluntary one. At this stage it relies on the co-operation of the landowner in question. There is, however, some incentive for a landowner to enter into an agreement in certain circumstances in the form of compensation. Under section 32 of WCA 1981, if a forestry or agricultural grant is refused because English Nature has objected to a project, English Nature must offer to enter into a management agreement. Such objection may result in refusal on the ground that the activities in question have destroyed, damaged or will destroy or damage flora or fauna or features by which the land is of special interest. In such a case English Nature must, within three months of receiving notice of the Secretary of State's refusal to offer grant aid, offer to enter into a management agreement. English Nature is obliged to submit to the owner or occupier a draft of an agreement into which he or she would be prepared to enter. The draft agreement may impose restrictions concerning the land and provide for payments to be made to the landowner or occupier as compensation for profit forgone or for reduced capital value which will accompany the agreement.

## Limits on compensation

Compensation as of right is limited to agriculture and forestry, a category of activities outside the normal planning legislation. A landowner that has planning permission refused or restrictive planning conditions attached to the issue of permission for reasons of nature conservation will not attract any compensation payments. This is despite a potential reduction in the value of the land.

## Financial guidelines

Circular 4/83 *(Financial Guidelines for Management Agreements)* provides for detailed procedures on negotiation of management agreements. Where English Nature is obliged to offer a draft agreement, that offer is usually in accordance with the guidance laid down in the Circular. The Circular states that any agreement should be as detailed as possible and should in any event record:

- the main heads of agreement, including the proposed restrictions and the period;
- the method of payment, if decided;
- if appropriate, the relevant standard payment: this refers to a situation where the agreement relates to a well-defined category of land and there will be restrictions on farming operations; a standard annual payment may be agreed and periodically revised, which may be more convenient and allow agreement to be reached more quickly;
- the sum(s) payable or how that figure is to be determined (i.e. by negotiation or arbitration); and
- if the agreement is not complete, a date not more than six months ahead by which a formal offer will be made.

## Operation of compensation regime

Operation of the regime is illustrated in two recent decisions, one of them a decision of the Scottish Lands Tribunal (*Cameron* v *Nature Conservancy Council* (1992) 9207 EG 128, 9208 EG 120 and 9209 EG 147). This case gives guidance on the basis for calculation of the amount of compensation. Mr Cameron owned a highland estate that contained two SSSIs making up some 30% of the total land area. He had hoped to implement a forestry scheme for the whole estate and sought aid from the Forestry Commission to carry this out. His application for a grant was refused on nature conservation grounds, the scheme being incompatible with the SSSI designations. In the absence of the grant from the Commission the proposed scheme was uneconomic and the NCC was obliged to offer compensation in the management agreement it negotiated, reflecting the decision to safeguard the conservation interest. Not surprisingly, the parties differed over the amount of compensation to be paid, so it fell to the Lands Tribunal to rule on the proper basis for compensation. Compensation was assessed at a figure being the difference between the open market value of the land without the SSSI designation and the open market value with the restrictions imposed by the management agreement. This accords with the guidance offered in Circular 4/83, which provides for the amount payable to be equal to the difference between the restricted and unrestricted value of the owner's or occupier's interest calculated in accordance with section 5 of the Land Compensation Act 1961.

The second case, *Thomas and another* v *Countryside Council for Wales* [1994] 4 All ER 853, also concerns the measure of compensation and the correct test for compensation for loss. The appellants were sheep farmers who exercised grazing rights over an area of cliff land, which was of particular value as it provided shelter for their sheep and was an important part of their sheep farming activity. The area was designated as an SSSI and the PDOs specified for the site required the appellants to drastically limit pasturing their sheep there. As a direct result of this the appellants radically altered their farming policy, reducing their flock and converting much of their land to arable use. Under the guidance in Circular 4/83 the compensation payment was agreed as an annual payment to reflect net profits foregone. An arbitrator appointed to settle a dispute concerning the correct level of compensation calculated the "net profits foregone" by reference to the difference between profits the appellants would have earned had they continued as before and the maximum income from the farm under the SSSI restrictions. In doing so the arbitrator rejected any claim for capital losses. On appeal, the Court of Appeal held that the basis for the measure of compensation under the guidelines was compensation for pecuniary loss which directly and naturally flowed. The court formulated a test for the compensation payable by asking:

(1) What could the landowner have achieved at the site?
(2) What had he achieved?
(3) Had any act or omission on the landowners part been unreasonable and of such a nature that the difference between (1) and (2) could not be said to have been caused by the restriction imposed? This question, the court held, should not be answered solely in terms of commercial optimum but should take some account of other circumstances, including individual personal factors of amenity or personal preference.

On the basis outlined above, the court held that the arbitrator's decision was wrong in law, since he failed to consider whether the adoption of the alternative farming policy was reasonable in the circumstances. Without this consideration the arbitrator had applied the wrong test for the capital losses claim. The award was remitted to him for reconsideration in the light of the court's ruling.

The court in *Thomas* held that the guidelines were intended to equate the manner of assessing compensation with the normal law applicable to cases of contractual or tortious liability. Under the normal law of contract and tort the fundamental basis for the measure of damages for compensation is the loss which naturally and directly flows from the breach. The qualification to this was only that the defendant would not be called upon to pay the full measure of damages unless he himself had acted reasonably to mitigate his loss. In other words, the plaintiff in any given situation would not be able to recover avoidable loss.

**Powers to conclude management agreements**

Management agreements are concluded by English Nature under powers available under section 16 of NPACA 1949 or section 15 of CA 1968. As mentioned above, these agreements are entirely voluntary and English Nature has no power to force a landowner to enter into such an agreement. If any such agreement is concluded (and it may be negotiated with the threat of a stronger, more effective nature conservation order designation being invoked if it cannot be successfully concluded), it may in the case of agricultural or forestry land entitle the landowner to compensation. This is calculated, as outlined above, on a profits foregone basis. Where no voluntary management agreement can be negotiated, an NCO may be made under section 29 of WCA 1981. These orders and their effect are considered below (see p 54); such orders can only be made by the Secretary of State.

Circular 4/83 provides that short-term agreements should be concluded to allow detailed negotiations to continue before settling a permanent agreement. Such an agreement is usually for a fixed term of between six and 12 months, and includes a commitment by the owner or occupier not to undertake the proposed operation while discussions on any subsequent long-term agreement continue. A nominal sum is payable on entering into a short-term agreement. For long-term agreements, owners or occupiers may choose either lump sum or annual payments.

**Effect of management agreement**

A management agreement is a legally binding enforceable contact. Its restrictive arrangements run with the land so that they can be enforced against successors in title (s 15(4)), but any positive arrangements for the site's management must be re-established with each owner by a new agreement. This is one of the recognised weaknesses of the regime: there is no effective provision for ensuring that positive obligations run with the land. A further difficulty may arise where no management agreement is in force as there can be no prohibition or restriction on the landowner simply doing nothing. In the case of certain outstanding nature conservation sites, positive management practices are necessary and doing nothing can be the most damaging operation. It is, however, one which cannot be listed in the schedule of PDOs. An example of this is the *London Brick Property* case (see p 44 above) where the ecological nature of the site would be destroyed unless the pumping of the site continued, an activity the company proposed to permanently discontinue. Thus any payment under a management agreement is not for positive conservation activities but for negative undertakings in the form of restraint from carrying out PDOs. This is the case even though a management agreement may provide for a positive obligation that can be enforced contractually against the party to it.

## 4.6 Nature conservation orders

**Purposes of NCOs**

These orders, which promote stronger protection than the SSSI designation alone, are made under section 29 of WCA 1981. An NCO may be made by the Secretary of State where it appears to him or her to be expedient to do so (s 29(1)(a)) for the purpose of:

- securing the survival in Great Britain of any kind of animal or plant or to comply with an international obligation, or
- conserving any of the land's flora, fauna or geological or physiographical features

where the land is, in the Secretary of State's opinion, of special interest or national importance. NCOs are sometimes referred to as "super SSSIs".

## Use of NCOs

NCOs have in fact been sparingly used. They have been used where situations are so serious as to require one to save an SSSI site from imminent destruction. However, there have been situations where the Secretary of State has refused to make an NCO despite the land already being designated an SSSI; it has occurred even where English Nature's advice is that the site should be so designated. Although NCOs appear superficially to be similar to SSSIs there are important differences and the restrictions imposed on the landowner are greater. On making an NCO under section 29 there may be an entitlement to compensation under section 30.

## The NCO-making procedure

NCOs are made under the procedure laid down in Schedule 11 to WCA 1981. An NCO comes into effect immediately it is made, unlike an SSSI designation which is confirmed within nine months. The owners, occupiers and LPA are then notified and it is publicised by means of advertisement in the local press and the *London Gazette* so that there is opportunity for objections to be made. This objection period runs for 28 days and objection is made to the Secretary of State, who is obliged under the procedures to appoint an inspector to hold a public inquiry if objections are not withdrawn. The inspector prepares a report to the Secretary of State who has the power to confirm, amend or revoke the NCO. There is provision within the schedule for the validity of orders to be questioned by way of judicial review. Any challenge to validity must be made within six weeks of the date of making the NCO.

**Effect of NCO**

In a similar fashion to SSSIs, an NCO contains a list of PDOs and the landowner is required to serve notice on English Nature where he or she intends to carry out a PDO. The landowner must then observe a three-month statutory ban on that operation during which time English Nature may take certain steps to protect or save the site. If English Nature opens negotiations on a management agreement or offers to enter into an agreement for the purchase of the site, the statutory ban on carrying out the operation is automatically extended from the SSSI period of four months to 12 months. This gives time for the conclusion of an agreement to save the feature of interest on the site. At the end of the extended statutory ban of 12 months the operation can go ahead if no agreement has been concluded, or on a date three months from rejection or withdrawal of the offer to enter into the agreement, whichever is the later.

What also makes the NCO designation more vigorous is the fact that an offence is committed where any person carries out a PDO without notifying English Nature or within the period of the statutory ban. An offence is committed regardless of whether that operation is carried out by the owner, occupier or a third party. This differs from the SSSI regime where only the owner or occupier may be prosecuted. This wider provision means that contractors, members of the public resorting to the land and even trespassers can be prosecuted under section 29(8) of WCA 1981.

English Nature has wider ancillary powers in relation to NCO land. Under section 51 of WCA 1981, English Nature may enter land to assess whether it should be subject to an order or to see if an offence has been committed. This power is not available where land is subject to an SSSI designation, a matter of some considerable concern to conservationists. It effectively means that an offence can be committed on SSSI land and, if not invited onto the land, English Nature has no way of verifying what may have occurred. There are proposals to amend legislation to extend the power for English Nature to enter land, outlined in the Government's consultation document *Sites of Special Scientific Interest* (see p 12).

Where an NCO designation is in existence, the court has an additional power to make a restoration order in respect of the land under section 31 of WCA 1981. This power is very often of little value where an offence has been committed which has resulted in the destruction of the feature of interest at the site. However, those at risk of prosecution should be mindful of the fact that the court can, if it convicts, insist on remediation measures in the form of a restoration order and that this may order specific works and involve expenditure. Compensation may also be payable to the owner or occupier for a reduction in the value of an agricultural holding as a result of making an order, and for any loss which arises directly from a ban on operations.

Unlike offences under section 28, where prosecution may only be brought by English Nature (unless an individual or organisation has the leave of the DPP), any interested party may bring a prosecution under section 29. This can mean a prosecution by the local authority or an interested conservation body such as the RSPB.

NCOs are sparingly used, but they do serve to allow English Nature additional time to conclude a management agreement for the site. In extreme cases they serve as notice of intent to use whatever powers are available to protect the site and may be an indication of English Nature's intention to compulsorily acquire the site, if possible.

Compulsory purchase is available to English Nature as a last resort if the land is considered to be of outstanding value. In rare instances this power has been employed to save a site. Compulsory purchase powers arise under section 17 of NPACA 1949. An order for compulsory purchase requires the Secretary of State's approval and, as noted above (see p 55), there have been occasions where the Secretary of State has refused to accept the advice of his or her statutory advisers, English Nature, and proceed with the compulsory purchase of a site.

## 4.7 Offences under SSSI and nature conservation order regimes

### SSSI offences

It is an offence for an owner or occupier, without reasonable excuse, to carry out or to cause or permit to be carried out a PDO in an SSSI under section 28(7) of WCA 1981. This applies unless the four-month statutory ban has elapsed or English Nature has given consent to the operation. A defendant is liable on summary conviction to a fine not exceeding level 4 on the standard scale (£2,500). The offence is one of strict liability.

Section 28 offences can only be prosecuted by English Nature so that it is not open to an interested party to bring a prosecution. This can only be done where the DPP's consent has been obtained under section 28(10). Two major weaknesses are also inherent in the legislation: first, the level of fine may be low enough to make commercial pressures for carrying out the PDO attractive even having regard to the risk of prosecution; secondly, the offence applies only to owners or occupiers of the land and not to the person responsible for the operation. This appears logical in the light of the fact that the duty on English Nature is to notify only owners or occupiers or those with an interest in the land of the SSSI designation. However, it can, as is illustrated in *Southern Water Authority* v *Nature Conservancy Council* [1992] 1 WLR 755, have disastrous consequences for the SSSI.

In *Southern Water* the NCC had designated an area of land on the Isle of Wight an SSSI. The site included a strip of land known as Hill Heath Ditch. Two farmers neighboured the ditch and both had been given notification of the designation and were aware of the PDOs applying to the site which were not to be carried out without the requisite consents being obtained or notification procedures being followed. It was a coincidence that Southern Water owned land within the SSSI and had been given notification in relation to the land in its ownership.

The farmers were anxious for the water authority to dredge the ditch, which was prone to flooding. There was some discussion between the NCC and the farmer owners about the proposal to dredge, but no agreement was reached nor permission given for operations to be carried out. The proposal to dredge was clearly a PDO in relation to this site, but no formal notice of an intention to carry it out was given to the NCC by the farmer owners of the site. The water authority nevertheless entered the site and commenced work on dredging the ditch, using an excavator to enlarge and reshape it, which in the process destroyed its ecological value.

For a reason that is not clear from the judgment, the water authority, and not the farmer owners, were prosecuted for carrying out a PDO at the site. On appeal, the House of Lords held that even though the water authority had been present at the site carrying out the works for some time, it did not constitute an "occupier" in the sense required under WCA 1981. It would seem that the prosecutor in this case chose to take action against the wrong party, as there seems no reason why a prosecution of the farmer owners for causing or permitting a PDO to be carried out would have fallen foul of the offence specified in the legislation. Lord Mustill, who gave the leading judgment, said that an occupier would be "someone who, although lacking the title of an owner nevertheless stands in such a comprehensive and stable relationship with the land as to be, in company with the actual owner, someone to whom the mechanisms can sensibly be made to apply. A stranger who entered the land for a few weeks solely to do some work on it does not fall into this category." From the judgment in *Southern Water* it is quite clear that categories of persons who may cause damage to a site's integrity (e.g. trespassers and flytippers) cannot face any legal consequences under section 28. Prosecution cannot occur for the offence of carrying out an operation in breach of the list of PDOs even where the person had knowledge of the designation and its list of PDOs.

Lord Mustill's comments on the SSSI regime in *Southern Water* are worth quoting. He described the water authority's acts as "ecological vandalism", but saved his harshest words for the regime itself:

> "It needs only a moment to see that this regime is toothless, for it demands no more from the owner or occupier of an SSSI than a little patience. Unless [the NCC] can convince the Secretary of State that the site is of sufficient national importance to justify an Order under section 29, a task rarely accomplished - the owner will within months be free to disregard the notification and carry out the proscribed operations no matter what the cost to the flora etc. on the site. In truth the Act does no more in the great majority of cases than give a breathing space within which to apply moral pressure, with a view to persuading the owner or occupier to make a voluntary agreement."

Since Lord Mustill's judgment the conservation regime has been strengthened where an SSSI is also subject to a designation under the Conservation (Natural Habitats, etc) Regulations which incorporate into English law the European Habitats Directive. An evaluation of the effect of the changes is given in Chapter 2.

**NCO offences**

Where a PDO has been carried out without consent in an area that is subject to an NCO, an offence may be committed under section 29(8) of WCA 1981. An offence under this section attracts on summary conviction a fine of the statutory maximum (£5,000) and an unlimited fine on indictment. In the case of a section 29(8) offence any person, and not just the owner or occupier, can be prosecuted. A prosecution under this section can be brought by an interested party, and is not limited to the statutory enforcing body, English Nature.

Under section 51 of WCA 1981, a power exists for English Nature to enter NCO land so that policing of the site may be more effective. There is also available to the court a power to issue a restoration order under section 31. This can require the offender to carry out specific works listed in the order to restore the land to its former condition. This may appear of limited use where the ecological value of the site has been destroyed, but may be of valuable assistance in preserving the site where damage limitation of one form or another can be carried out. In addition to this, if a restoration order is not complied with within the time laid down in it, English Nature may enter the land, carry out the work and recover the expenses of doing so from the offender under section 31(6).

**Proposals for reform**

Proposals are under consideration for the amendment of legislation and administrative changes to better protect SSSIs. A consultation document, *Sites of Special Scientific Interest: Better Protection and Management*, was issued in September 1998 outlining proposed changes. An outline of the proposals appears at p 12.

**Key points**

*Designation*

- English Nature has a *duty* to designate SSSIs under WCA 1981.
- English Nature is obliged to notify designation of a site to every owner and occupier and the LPA.
- Any SSSI notification contains a list of PDOs.
- The landowner may be granted specific permission to carry out a PDO; if not he or she can carry out a PDO on expiry of four months from his or her giving notice.

*Planning permission*

- Designation as an SSSI does not remove the need for planning permission.

- The LPA is obliged to consult English Nature on any application within an SSSI.
- English Nature may request that the Secretary of State call in the application for consideration.
- English Nature's representations to the LPA are a material consideration.
- If planning permission is granted it overrides the SSSI designation.

*Management agreements and compensation*

- An SSSI designation is registered as a local land charge.
- Agreement to refrain from a forestry or agricultural activity may attract compensation.
- Circular 4/83 (Financial Guidelines for Management Agreements) provides detailed procedures for these agreements.

*NCOs*

- These are made under section 29 of WCA 1981.
- They are sparingly used, but have been used to save SSSIs from imminent destruction.
- They are made under the procedures laid down in Schedule 11 to WCA 1981.
- There is a three-month statutory ban on carrying out PDOs which is automatically extended to 12 months if English Nature opens negotiations on a management agreement.
- An offence can be committed by any person, not just the owner or occupier.
- English Nature has wider ancillary powers in relation to NCOs (*e.g.* to enter land).
- Compulsory purchase may be used if the land is of outstanding value under section 17 of NPACA 1949.
- It is a strict liability offence for an owner or occupier to carry out or to cause or permit to be carried out a PDO in an SSSI; on summary conviction this attracts a fine not exceeding level 4 on the standard scale.
- Where an NCO is in force, a fine not exceeding level 5 applies and an unlimited fine on indictment.

*Chapter 5*

# Other UK Nature
# · Conservation Designations ·

The designations considered in this chapter are no less important to, but are not as familiar as, those considered in previous chapters. The local authority's ability to require public access to the countryside is also considered.

## *5.1* National nature reserves (NNRs)

### Basis for designation

NNRs are defined as areas managed for study or research into flora, fauna or of geological or physiographical interest, or for preserving such features which are of special interest. They are designated by English Nature under section 19 of NPACA 1949 or section 35 of WCA 1981. The designation procedure is not complicated: English Nature simply declares an area an NNR if it considers it is expedient in the national interest to manage the area as one. All NNRs are also designated as SSSIs.

Questions of what constitutes the national interest have been considered in the courts. Any decision to declare an area an NNR can only be challenged by way of judicial review on the basis that English Nature's declaration was unreasonable, ultra vires or flawed in some other respect. It was held in *Re Amalgamated Anthracite Collieries Ltd's Application* (1927) 43 TLR 672 that whether a thing is in the national interest is a question of fact at the time. It is to be decided in the light of all the circumstances and conditions as they exist at that time, notwithstanding that they would not have been specifically envisaged by the legislature when an Act was passed (*Cartwright* v *Post Office* [1968] 2 All ER 646). In the light of recent concern for conservation, this judgment seems to favour any declaration made by English Nature rather than an individual landowner.

**What is an NNR?**

What distinguishes NNRs from other nature conservation designations is that English Nature must have "control" of a site in order to designate it as such. It is English Nature, rather than the owner or occupier, that manages the site as an NNR. For English Nature to have sufficient control to permit designation it must either own or have a long lease of the land or have entered into a legally enforceable agreement with the owner (a nature reserve agreement). Such agreement is made under section 16 of NPACA 1949 and is legally enforceable against successors in title to the land. An extension to the section 16 provisions was introduced by section 35 of WCA 1981, which permits English Nature to designate an NNR on land controlled, owned and managed by an "approved body", defined as a voluntary conservation organisation, such as the RSPB.

**Nature reserve agreements**

A nature reserve agreement under section 16 may:

(1) impose restrictions on the exercise of rights over the land by those who have an interest in it;
(2) provide for the management of the land in a specified manner or carrying out work on the land in connection with its management, as is considered necessary;
(3) make provision for payment for any works provided for under the agreement by the owner, third parties or English Nature or for the expenses to be shared by all or any of them; and
(4) make provision for compensation payments against restrictions in the agreement.

**Compulsory purchase powers**

Powers of compulsory purchase are available to English Nature with the Secretary of State's approval. These powers can be used if it is not possible to conclude a satisfactory management agreement, or where an existing agreement has been breached. In practice, powers of compulsory purchase are very rarely exercised, but they may be used in isolated cases where English Nature is unable to persuade a landowner to enter into a nature reserve agreement or to relinquish ownership of the site. Compulsory purchase powers are available under section 17 of NPACA 1949, subsection (2) of which emphasises that the powers are a method of last resort. It provides that English Nature shall not acquire any interest in land unless it is satisfied that it cannot conclude agreement terms necessary to secure that the land is satisfactorily managed as a nature reserve.

## Protections for NNRs

Surprisingly, no extra legal protections arise where land is NNR designated. The site's legal protection comes from its SSSI designation, not its NNR status. What additional protection is necessary is provided for in any nature reserve agreement terms in force in respect of the site or by the fact that it is in English Nature's ownership. The fact that English Nature or an approved body controls the site effectively limits the danger of damage to the site. Damage usually occurs from third party activities and NPACA 1949 helps English Nature to avoid this as much as possible by conferring a power to make byelaws in respect of an NNR site. This can assist in the site's management and enables penalties to be imposed for certain undesirable activities. Section 20 specifically provides that byelaws made may address the following:

(1) restricted entry to or movement within nature reserves of people, vehicles, boats or animals;
(2) killing, taking or disturbing fauna within the nature reserve, taking or interfering with any flora in the reserve, and destroying or disturbing eggs;
(3) prohibiting or restricting shooting birds or birds in the surrounding or adjoining area as English Nature thinks necessary for the protection of the reserve;
(4) depositing rubbish and leaving litter in the area;
(5) prohibiting lighting fires, or anything likely to cause a fire;
(6) issuing permits for entry into the reserve or for any other activity which would otherwise be unlawful; and
(7) restricting any of the above activities in any limited area of the reserve; this allows byelaws to apply in relation to a particular area of the reserve without restricting that activity on the whole of it.

Byelaws are subject to the Secretary of State's approval. They are made under procedures in the Local Government Act 1972 as if English Nature were a local authority by virtue of section 106 of NPACA 1949.

## 5.2 National parks (NPs)

### Status of NPs

NPs have a special place in the planning regime, overseen by the national park authority (NPA) which acts as the planning authority for the area. An NPA is the only example in UK conservation law of an autonomous institutional structure set up with a specific brief to protect and conserve the countryside. Section 67 of the Environment Act 1995 inserted a new section 4A into TCPA 1990, which provides for the NPA to be the sole LPA for the area. The NPA therefore assumes all the planning functions of a local authority in connection with the NP.

### Purpose of NPs

The legislation relating to NPs was updated and amended by the Environment Act 1995. NP designation can apply to vast areas of land subject to occupation by thousands of people, and is made under section 5 of NPACA 1949 as substituted by the Environment Act 1990. Section 5(1) sets out the purpose of NP designated areas as:

"(a) conserving and enhancing the natural beauty, wildlife and cultural heritage of the areas; and
(b) promoting opportunities for the understanding and enjoyment of the special qualities of those areas by the public."

The "areas" referred to in subparagraph (a) above are described in NPACA 1949 as:

"those extensive tracts of countryside in England that by reason of–
(a) their natural beauty and
(b) the opportunities they afford for open-air recreation, having regard both to their character and to their position in relation to centres of population

it is especially desirable that the necessary measures are taken to conserve and enhance and promote opportunities for public enjoyment."

What is apparent from this definition is that NPs are a designation concerned with amenity, and not just conservation. However, public bodies and statutory undertakers are obliged where there is conflict between purposes (a) and (b) in section 5(1) to give greater weight to purpose (a), so that conservation is the uppermost consideration. This is enshrined in NPACA 1949 itself by means of new section 11A, inserted into the Act by the Environment Act 1995. NPAs are under a duty to balance environmental factors with economic and amenity considerations to seek to foster economic and social well-being of local communities within the NP. NPs are living and working communities and not just areas where conservation of the natural environment is paramount.

## Procedure on designation

The Countryside Agency is responsible for new NP designations. The National Parks Commission under NPACA 1949 designated the 10 original parks in the 1950s. There is discussion concerning designation of further areas as NPs; this would require designation under section 5(3) of NPACA 1949 and must be by statutory instrument, which is confirmed by the Secretary of State. The 10 NPs in existence at present are the Brecon Beacons, Dartmoor, Exmoor, the Lake District, the North Yorkshire Moors, Northumberland, the Peak District, the Pembrokeshire Coast, Snowdonia and the Yorkshire Dales. Any further designations will be made under section 5(3) and follow procedures laid down in Schedule 1 to NPACA 1949. This includes an opportunity for objection to the proposed designation. If an objection is made and is not withdrawn, the Secretary of State may direct that a public local inquiry be held to consider the draft order. He or she may confirm the order with or without modifications.

## NPAs

The make up of NPAs is governed by the Environment Act 1995. Section 63 empowers the Secretary of State to establish by order an NPA. The NPA's composition is set out in Schedule 7 to the Act, which also sets out its duties and functions. Schedule 7 states that an NPA is a body corporate and confers on it a similar status to local authorities.

The 1995 Act has the effect of converting what were bodies run and administered by local authorities into bodies with local authority status in their own right. NPAs are now subject to many of the requirements of local authorities, including requirements of transparency and the jurisdiction of the Ombudsman. The county and district councils appoint half of the NPA members plus two additional members; the remainder are directly appointed by the Secretary of State after consultation with the Countryside Agency. The exact number of members of each authority is provided for in the statutory instrument setting up the NPA.

### Countryside Agency's role

The Countryside Agency has a duty to give advice to the appropriate planning authorities (usually the NPA) on the arrangements to be made for administering the area as an NP. It is also obliged to assist the authorities to carry out their functions under NPACA 1949 to provide access for open-air recreation and facilities for the public visiting the NP. A further duty is imposed on the Agency to give advice to the Secretary of State on proposals for development in an NP. It must also advise the LPA in connection with the preparation or amendment of a development plan, or in connection with a planning application in an NP. If any proposals appear to the Agency to be inconsistent with the NP's maintenance it may make recommendations to the Secretary of State for proposals for development. All these duties are outlined in section 6 of NPACA 1949. It is also incumbent on all NPAs to prepare and update every five years a map of their park conforming to guidelines issued by the Agency showing any areas the NPA regards as particularly important to preserve (WCA 1981, s 43). The purpose of such a map is to assist in strategic planning for the NP of any area of particular significance. Under section 43(3) the map is to apply to any mountain, moor, heath, woodland, down, cliff or foreshore or land adjacent to the foreshore.

### How NP protections arise

The protections afforded to NPs arise through the planning system administered by the NPA. It is sensitive and sympathetic planning, rather than any specific nature conservation protections, that afford protection in an NP. Each NP has a development plan and a management plan. Management plans were originally prepared under the Local Government Act 1972 requirements, but are now required under section 66 of the Environment Act 1995. These plans formulate policies for carrying out the NPA's functions and management responsibilities. The development plan, on the other hand, is a planning document in the same sense as a local authority development plan. Planning decisions in the NP are made in accordance with the plan as provided for by section 54A of TCPA 1990, unless there are other material considerations that override the plan. In NPs the planning regime is paramount in protecting the park's integrity. Government guidance to local authorities, PPG7, also gives advice on NP planning policy (see further pages 120-122).

Damaging activities, such as quarrying and peat cutting, are undertaken in NPs, very often the result of historical legacies which commenced before conservation was an issue within the planning process. Such activities cannot be rescinded under the planning system. If an activity is already lawfully being carried out in an NP the only remedy available to an NPA is to seek a discontinuance order under section 102 of TCPA 1990. This is a course of action which, in the case of a profitable business, is usually prohibitively expensive because of the compensation to be paid under section 115 of TCPA 1990 on making the order. A discontinuance order also requires the Secretary of State's confirmation under section 103 of the 1990 Act. An NPA may review any development plan as provided under TCPA 1990. The management plan is also subject to review every five years under the provisions of section 66(4) of the Environment Act 1995.

For its funding, an NPA issues a levy to councils which make up the NPA's members. Sections 71-74 of the Environment Act 1995 govern NPA finances and include powers for the Secretary of State to make grants to an NPA on such terms and conditions as he or she thinks fit. It is current government policy for 75% of an NPA's funding to be met through central government grants; the levy on constituent councils making up the authority provides the difference.

## 5.3 Areas of outstanding natural beauty (AONBs)

**Designation**

AONBs are designated by English Nature under section 87 of NPACA 1949. They are designated by order, which must be confirmed by the Secretary of State. The designation is complementary to a national park designation and certain provisions of NPACA 1949 are applied to AONBs by section 88 of that Act.

English Nature may declare an area an AONB where it is not in a national park and it is of the view that an area is of such outstanding natural beauty that the NPACA 1949 protections should apply. Under section 87(2), English Nature is obliged to consult with all local authorities whose area includes part of the proposed AONB. It must also publish notice of the intention to declare an AONB in the *London Gazette* and in at least one local newspaper circulating in the proposed area. The notice must indicate the effect of the proposed order and state the period for objections to the proposed designation and the manner in which they may be made. Objections are usually required to be made to English Nature in writing, and English Nature and the Secretary of State must consider any representation made before confirming the order. The Secretary of State may confirm the order with or without modifications. Copies of an AONB order must be made available to the public for inspection at all reasonable hours at the offices of English Nature and each local authority whose area includes the AONB.

**Protections applying to AONBs**

By means of section 88 of NPACA 1949, certain provisions of that Act are applied to AONBs. This means that AONBs attract some of the same protections as an area designated as a national park. English Nature is obliged to give advice to the Secretary of State on any proposals for development in an AONB (s 6(4)(e)) and may make representations to the local authorities responsible for preparing the development plan for the AONB. In addition the local authority is obliged to consult with English Nature in relation to access agreements negotiated in respect of the land. Essentially, as in NPs, the AONB relies on the Town and Country Planning Acts for its protection and enhancement. Government guidance on planning policy in AONBs is contained in PPG7.

The important difference between NPs and AONBs is that AONBs are afforded their protections via the planning system by the local authority for the area. They do not have the additional protection of a planning authority charged with NPA duties. Consequently, AONB protection relies solely on the LPA. No additional finance is allocated to LPAs to carry out their planning functions with specific regard to AONBs, a further weakness of the protections.

## *5.4* **Limestone pavements**

Under section 34 of WCA 1981, English Nature is under a duty to notify the LPA where it is of the opinion that land which comprises a limestone pavement is of special interest by reason of its flora, fauna or geological or physiographical features. This means that the limestone pavement area is protected through the town and country planning system. A "limestone pavement" is defined in the legislation (s 34(6)) as "an area of limestone, which lies wholly or partly exposed on the surface of the ground and has been fissured by natural erosion".

If the character or appearance of any land notified to the LPA would be likely to be adversely affected by the limestone's removal or interference with it, the county planning authority or the Secretary of State may make a limestone pavement order. Such an order prohibits the removal or disturbance of limestone on the land. The procedures for making a limestone pavement order are the same as those governing the designation of an SSSI and are set out in Schedule 11 to WCA 1981. The owners and occupiers of the area of the proposed order are notified and the order is publicised by advertisement in the local press and the *London Gazette* so that there is opportunity for objections to be made. This objection period runs for 28 days and the notice itself specifies the manner in which objections should be made. If they are made and are not withdrawn, the Secretary of State may hold a public local inquiry. An inspector appointed to consider the representations prepares a report of his or her findings for the Secretary of State who may confirm the order with or without modifications or may revoke it as he or she thinks fit.

It is an offence without reasonable excuse to remove or disturb limestone on or in any land designated by a limestone pavement order. On summary conviction before the magistrates the penalty may be a fine up to the statutory maximum (£5,000) or on indictment an unlimited fine. As with land in an SSSI, it is a defence to any prosecution where a valid planning permission exists for the activity.

## 5.5 Marine nature reserves (MNRs)

MNRs are designated under section 36 of WCA 1981. They are made by the Secretary of State on English Nature's recommendation, which makes application to the Secretary of State for certain lands and waters to be managed by it. MNRs are the counterpart to NNRs. In the case of MNRs the designation applies to "any land covered (continuously or intermittently) by tidal waters or parts of the sea". The definition of "sea" is a distance of 12 nautical miles landward or seaward of the baselines from which the breadth of the territorial sea adjacent to Great Britain is measured. The baselines for the measurement of territorial sea are established by Order in Council (see Territorial Sea Act 1987, s 1). In reality this means that MNRs do not always extend to a great distance, allowing for tides and the fact that large areas of land are intermittently under water.

### Purpose of MNRs

MNRs cover areas that, in English Nature's opinion, should be managed by English Nature to:

(1) conserve marine flora or fauna or geological or physiographical features of special interest in the area; or
(2) provide, under suitable conditions and control, special opportunities for studying, and research into, matters relating to marine flora and fauna and the physical conditions in which they live, or for studying geological and physiographical features of special interest in the area.

English Nature may manage an area for either or both of the above purposes (WCA 1981, s 36). English Nature will regulate the MNR by means of byelaws, which accompany, in draft, any application for an order to the Secretary of State (s 36(2)) and any order proposed will follow the procedures set out in Schedule 12 to WCA 1981, the same schedule for making NCOs. Under Schedule 12, notice must be given of the Secretary of State's intention to make the order and copies of the order and any draft byelaws must be made available for public inspection. Notice must be given by publication in the *London Gazette* and at least one local newspaper circulating in the area of the proposed order. Objections to the order may be made by the date specified in the notice, not less than 28 days from the date of publication of the notice of intention. If an objection is made and is not withdrawn, the Secretary of State is obliged before making the order to hold a public local inquiry or hearing. He or she may then make the order with or without modifications. An order's validity may be questioned after it has been made by way of judicial review on grounds that it is not made within the powers of section 36 or the Secretary of State has not followed the designated procedures laid down in Schedule 12.

### MNR byelaws

Byelaws for protecting MNRs are made with the Secretary of State's consent under section 37 of WCA 1981. Section 37(2) sets out the scope of such byelaws. This is not as extensive as those relating to NNRs under section 20 of NPACA 1949 and has an important limitation in that they may not restrict commercial shipping. The section itself also limits the restrictions on pleasure boats. Section 37(3) provides that byelaws under section 37 may not:

(1) prohibit or restrict the exercise of any right of passage by a vessel other than a pleasure boat; or
(2) prohibit, except for particular parts of the reserve at particular times of the year, the exercise of any such right by a pleasure boat.

English Nature has the right under section 36(6) to install markers indicating the existence and extent of an MNR. Note, however, that the powers available to English Nature do not extend to interference with the functions of certain statutory bodies including the NRA, a water or sewerage undertaker, an internal drainage board, a navigation authority and a harbour authority.

## 5.6 **European marine sites**

The Conservation (Natural Habitats, etc) Regulations 1994 extend to European marine sites as well as European sites. A European marine site is defined in the Regulations as a European site which consists of, or so far as it consists of, marine areas. Marine areas are also defined as areas of land covered (continuously or intermittently) by tidal waters or any part of the sea in or adjacent to Great Britain up to the seaward limit of territorial waters. European sites include areas classified under the Birds Directive as SPAs. These have particular significance, as they are frequently coastal areas supporting wading and waterfowl populations. These areas are now subjected to the additional controls of the Habitats Regulations by virtue of their designation as European marine sites.

Under regulation 33 of the Habitats Regulations, "the appropriate nature conservation body" (*i.e.* English Nature) has power to install markers indicating the existence and extent of a European marine site. It also has a duty under regulation 33(3) to advise other relevant authorities (which specifically includes both the local authority and any harbour authority for the area) about:

(1) the site's conservation objectives; and
(2) any operations which may cause deterioration of natural habitats or the habitats of species, or disturbance of species for which the site has been designated.

**Management schemes for European marine sites**

Regulation 35 contains important powers for those authorities listed in regulation 5. These include county and district councils, the NRA, water undertakers and sewerage undertakers, internal drainage boards, navigation authorities and harbour authorities. Under regulation 35 the Secretary of State, alone or jointly with the Minister of Agriculture, Fisheries and Food, may give directions to the "relevant authorities" listed there in establishing a management scheme for a European marine site. These directions may, in particular:

(1) require conservation measures to be included in the scheme;
(2) appoint one of the relevant authorities to co-ordinate its establishment;
(3) set time limits within which steps are to be taken;
(4) provide that the Secretary of State's approval is required before the scheme is established; and
(5) require any authority to supply the Secretary of State with such information as he or she may require in the direction.

There is also a power for the Secretary of State, or the Secretary of State jointly with the Minister of Agriculture, Fisheries and Food, to give directions for the amendment of any management scheme.

Regulation 35 gives wide powers to require a management scheme to be established. The regulation is rather vague in its provision and academics have questioned whether it is a true implementation of the Habitats Directive. In practice, English Nature will advise the other relevant authorities on the nature conservation needs of an area. English Nature will hope to agree management schemes with other authorities. However, it would be within the Secretary of State's powers to direct, for example, that any local authority in the area of a European marine site or any harbour authority for the area responsible for the additional administrative and financial burden of co-ordinating a management scheme. Powers to direct that a scheme be implemented within a specific time frame may be an added burden. In all probability the regulation will be used where it is necessary to require the co-operation of authorities with potentially conflicting aims. This could arise where, for example, a body such as a harbour authority, which holds the interests of commercial shipping paramount, has jurisdiction over an area and English Nature is concerned with the preservation of the special interest of an area.

## 5.7 Local nature reserves

Local authorities may establish these under section 21 of NPACA 1949, which permits a local authority to provide or to secure the provision of nature reserves on land in its area, where it appears expedient that it should be managed as a nature reserve. Section 21(2) applies the provisions of NPACA 1949 as respects NNRs to a local authority by providing that references in the Act to English Nature should be read as references to a local authority. The section also provides that where references in NPACA 1949 are to "the national interest", in the case of local nature reserves they shall be to "the interests of the locality".

There is one check on a local authority's ability to designate a local nature reserve contained in NPACA 1949, in that it is obliged under section 21(6) to exercise its functions in relation to local nature reserves in consultation with English Nature. Once a local reserve is designated, the local authority may make agreements for establishing local nature reserves, and have powers of compulsory purchase available in the event that an agreement is not adhered to. It also has powers to make byelaws in respect of a local nature reserve.

## 5.8 **Other designations**

### Green belt

Although not strictly a nature conservation designation, a green belt can in certain circumstances prevent development to the benefit of nature conservation. The law in this area is detailed and complex, and where a potential development site is in green belt land a careful study of the appropriate local and national planning guidance is necessary. In the majority of cases development is labelled inappropriate development and very special circumstances must be established to justify development being granted permission.

Green belt is one of the oldest and best known planning designations for land. Originally established as a planning designation in 1955, the purpose of green belt policy is to prevent urban sprawl by keeping land permanently open. As included in the stated purposes, a green belt assists in safeguarding the countryside from encroachment. Once land is designated green belt, the main objectives are to provide the urban population with opportunities for access to open countryside, to retain attractive landscapes, to enhance landscapes near to where people live and to secure nature conservation interest. These policy objectives often ensure that green belt land is protected from development. Government policy on the development of green belt land is contained in PPG2 and is strict. It provides that with regard to development in the green belt there will be a general presumption against inappropriate development within it. Such development should not be approved and will not normally be permitted unless it falls within certain specified categories of development, or the applicant can show very special circumstances for it to be permitted. Consideration of PPG2 is to be found at page 122 below.

### Geological conservation review sites

These sites are not a stand alone designation, but are included in SSSI designation notification as a result of a survey of such sites carried out by the former NCC. The survey identified sites where conservation is essential because of unique features of geological interest. PPG9 refers to conservation of such sites being essential for education and research in the earth sciences.

## *5.9* **Access agreements and orders**

Part V of NPACA 1949 deals with access to open country. Its provisions are extended in CA 1968. Section 64 of NPACA 1949 provides: "A local planning authority may make an access agreement with any person having an interest in land, being open country, in the area of the authority."

The aim of the legislation is to enable access agreements to be concluded to allow public access to open countryside for open-air recreation. This is achieved by means of an access agreement or access order. Alternatively, land may be acquired under the Act to afford public access.

### Definition of "open country"

"Open country" is defined in section 59 of NPACA 1949 and has been extended by CA 1968. It means any area appearing to the LPA to consist wholly or predominately of mountain, moor, heath, down, cliff or foreshore. The CA 1968 extended this to include woodlands, river or canal and a strip of land adjacent on both sides of a river or canal. Section 16 of CA 1968 provides that the strip of land comprised in any access order must be wide enough to allow public access on foot along the water, and to allow the public to picnic at convenient places and, where practicable, to embark and disembark. The LPA is obliged under the CA 1968 provisions to exercise its powers under Part V over any such strip of land with special regard to persons using small boats (*e.g.* rowing boats, canoes) who have to circumvent obstacles on the water by passing round on foot with their boats.

Where the LPA intends to make any access agreement on land adjacent to a river or canal, it is obliged to consult with and seek the consent of the Environment Agency and other authorities having functions in relation to the river or canal. The provisions of CA 1968 dealing with canals do not extend to waters owned or managed by British Waterways.

### Procedure on making access orders

An access order must be submitted to the Secretary of State for confirmation. Schedule 1 to NPACA 1949 sets out the procedure for making and confirming access orders. The procedures include giving public notice of an intention to make the order, an opportunity for objections to be made and, where any such objection is not withdrawn, holding a possible public inquiry into making the order. Making an access order attracts compensation (s 70) where the value of a person's interest is depreciated in consequence of the order. However, for compensation payment to be made an owner is obliged under section 71 to wait until the order has been in operation for five years. This allows compensation to be assessed in the light of experience gained of the order's actual effect. If an access agreement is made it may provide for making compensation payments in consideration of making the agreement and/or by way of contribution towards expenditure incurred by the person making the agreement as a consequence of it (NPACA 1949, s 64).

Section 67 of NPACA 1949 provides that access agreements and orders may make such provision as appears expedient for securing that sufficient access to the land in the order or agreement is available to the public. The order or agreement itself may contain provision for:

(1) improving or repairing existing accesses to the land;
(2) constructing any new access necessary;
(3) restricting interference by the owner with accesses to the land and other activities which may result in interference; and
(4) maintaining any such access.

The LPA may contribute to or pay the entire cost of any works provided for in the agreement or order. It may also make contributions or pay for maintenance of the access to the land.

If the LPA fails to secure a satisfactory agreement with the landowner, or if the owner or occupier fails to carry out works provided for in the agreement, the LPA may carry out the works itself, having given notice of its intention to do so. The power in section 67(5) also extends to allow the LPA to recover costs of works in certain circumstances. In a case where the LPA is obliged only to make a contribution to costs, it may recover the remaining costs from the person who by virtue of the agreement was obliged to meet a share of them. The LPA must show that the costs incurred by it were reasonable and can only take such action where the owner or occupier failed to carry out the works within a reasonable time. What is reasonable depends on the circumstances of each case.

If land is subject to an access agreement or an access order, its owner is prohibited from carrying out work on the land which substantially reduces public access. In certain circumstances the LPA is entitled to enforce access under section 68 of NPACA 1949 by serving a notice requiring the owner or occupier to restore or re-open any means of access, or to provide a new means of access. If he or she fails to comply with such notice, the LPA may carry out the necessary works itself and recover the costs from him or her.

**Proposals for reform**

Proposals are under consideration to grant a general statutory right of access to open countryside. A document issued by the Government in March 1999, *Access to the Countryside: The Government's Framework for Action*, sets out the proposals. These are considered in more detail at page 13.

**Key points**

- English Nature declares an area an NNR if it considers it expedient in the national interest to do so. It always has "control" of an NNR site either by ownership or nature reserve agreement. It may make byelaws to ensure the site's protection.
- No extra protections arise where land is designated an NNR.
- National parks are administered by national park authorities which are also the planning authority for the area. National parks are designated for amenity and conservation purposes. The Countryside Agency advises on the administration of the national park.
- Section 88 of NPACA 1949 applies certain provisions to AONBs so that they attract some of the same protections as an NP designated area. Such protections arise through the planning system and rely solely on the LPA.
- English Nature notifies an LPA where land that comprises a limestone pavement is of special interest. Protections afforded to limestone pavements arise through the planning system.
- Marine nature reserves are designated under section 36 WCA 1981; they are the marine counterpart to NNRs. They are managed by byelaws which may not restrict commercial shipping.

- English Nature will advise other relevant authorities for the area of the conservation objectives for a European marine site and any operations which may cause deterioration of natural habitats or the habitats of species for which the site has been designated. Management schemes may be established for a European marine site.
- Local nature reserves can be established by local authorities under NPACA 1949 provisions.
- The legislation allows access agreements to be concluded to enable public access for open air recreation to open countryside. Making an access order attracts compensation where the value of a landowner's interest is depreciated as a result of it.
- Where land is subject to an access order its owner is prohibited from carrying out work on it that results in substantially reduced public access.

# Chapter 6
# Protection of Individual · Species and Plants ·

## 6.1 Wild birds

The protections for wild birds are contained in WCA 1981. Under section 1 it is an offence to kill, injure or take any wild bird. It is also an offence to take, damage or destroy a bird's nest when it is in use or being built and to take or destroy an egg of any wild bird. To be in possession of a wild bird or one of its eggs, even where the bird is dead or the egg will not hatch, also falls within the provisions (s 1(1) and (2)). *Kirkland* v *Robinson* [1987] 1 JP 377 established that the possession of birds is a strict liability offence and that a person commits the offence when he or she takes possession of the item or thing in question.

### Scheme of protection

The WCA 1981 divides bird protection by means of two schedules to the Act. Both the common and Latin names of each bird are listed in the schedules. These schedules are reviewed every five years and local authorities notified of any amendments and additions for planning purposes. The Secretary of State has power under section 22 to add birds to or remove them from the schedules. Schedule 1 lists the rarer species of bird to which stronger enforcement penalties apply; the Schedule 1 provisions are extended to cover disturbance of dependant young of any such bird. A bird listed in the Schedule is presumed to be wild in all circumstances unless it can be proved otherwise. Intentionally disturbing a Schedule 1 bird on or near its nest, or disturbing its dependant young, is an offence under section 5(2) and attracts a penalty up to level 5 on the standard scale (£5,000). In the case of other birds, a fine not exceeding level 3 on the standard scale (£1,000) may be imposed. Section 18 makes it an offence to attempt to commit an offence under Part I of the Act. Part I includes all the offences referred to above.

Schedule 2 to the Act contains a list of species of wildfowl bird which it is permitted to kill or take outside the closed season. The "closed season" is defined in section 2(4), although the Secretary of State has power to amend the closed season for any bird by order. He or she also has powers to vary the closed season and, if it is necessary to provide special protection for any species in any particular year, to declare any period (not exceeding 14 days) as one of special protection for those birds. Any order providing special protection for any species has the effect of extending the closed season for that species. The closed season is intended to allow birds shot for sport a period for breeding and regeneration.

## Definition of "wild bird"

Wild birds are defined by section 27 of WCA 1981 as any bird of a kind that is ordinarily resident in or is a visitor to Great Britain in a wild state. The definition specifically excludes poultry and, except in relation to certain offences relating to methods of taking any bird and licences for certain specified purposes, game birds. Game birds are variously defined in statute but include pheasant, partridge and grouse or moor game, black or heath game or ptarmigan. Various statutes governing game such as the Game Act 1831, the Game Licences Act 1860 and the Ground Game Acts 1880 and 1906 protect these birds.

## Offences of taking or killing

The offence prohibiting certain methods of taking or killing wild birds, which applies to all wild birds including those defined as game and those where killing or taking is permitted outside the closed season, is contained in section 5 of WCA 1981. The section provides that it is an offence liable to a special penalty (up to a £5,000 fine) to:

(1) set in position any article which will cause bodily injury to a wild bird (*i.e.* a springe, trap, gin, snare, hook and line, any electrical device for killing, stunning or frightening, or any poisonous, poisoned or stupefying substance);
(2) use any such articles or any net, bait board, bird-lime or similar substance;

(3) use to kill or take any wild bird:
  (a) a bow or crossbow;
  (b) explosives;
  (c) an automatic or semi-automatic weapon;
  (d) a shot gun where the barrel has an internal diameter of more than one and three quarter inches;
  (e) a device for illuminating a target or for night shooting;
  (f) artificial lighting, a mirror or other dazzling device;
  (g) gas or smoke; or
  (h) a chemical wetting agent;
(4) use as a decoy any sound recording, live bird or other animal which is tethered or secured by other means, or which is blind, maimed or injured;
(5) use any mechanically propelled vehicle in immediate pursuit of a wild bird to kill or take it; or
(6) knowingly cause or permit any of the above acts to be done.

Part II of Schedule 2 to the Act lists species of pest bird. These birds fall outside of any protections and they may be killed or taken, or their nests or eggs destroyed by the owner of the land on which they are situated. There is also provision for these birds to be taken by any other authorised person. "Authorised person" is defined in section 27 of WCA 1981 to cover persons authorised by the landowner or occupier where the action to destroy the birds or their eggs is taken. This covers a situation where, for example, an outside contractor is employed to destroy pest birds' eggs. The local authority for the area may also authorise action to be taken, as may English Nature and the Environment Agency. However, any authorisation does not confer powers to enter the land on which the action is proposed to be taken; permission from the landowner must also be obtained.

Under section 21(6), if a court convicts an offender under Part I of WCA 1981 it may also order forfeiture of any bird, nest or egg.

**Bird sanctuaries**

Areas of special protection are provided for under section 3 of WCA 1981. These areas are not to be confused with SPAs under the Birds Directive (see p 16 above); they are a separate designation, although the two may overlap. The WCA 1981 allows the Secretary of State to make provision for any area to have special protection as a bird sanctuary.

The section expressly provides that making any such order does not affect the exercise by any person of any right he or she may have as owner or occupier. The Secretary of State is also obliged to have obtained the consent of all the landowners and occupiers (s 3(5)). He or she must give particulars of the intended order either by notice in writing to every owner and occupier to be included in the area of the order, or by advertising in a newspaper circulating in the district in which that area is situated. The requirements for advertisement do not, interestingly, require advertisement in a local newspaper; an advertisement in a national paper is sufficient. A period of three months must be given to allow objections to the proposed order to be made. The opportunity for objection is only available under the WCA 1981 provisions to landowners and occupiers affected by the order; it is not an opportunity for general objections to making the order.

### Exceptions to restrictions on taking or killing

Section 4 of WCA 1981 provides for exceptions to sections 1 and 3. It is under this section that one of the most important practical implications of the legislation arises. Section 4(2)(c) provides that notwithstanding the restrictions on taking and killing wild birds in section 1, or the provisions of any order made under section 3, in certain designated situations a person will not be guilty of an offence. One such situation is "any act made unlawful by those provisions [which] was the incidental result of a lawful operation and could not reasonably have been avoided". This provides an important defence for those who carry out development and have planning permission for their operations. For example, where the removal of trees and hedging is required to carry out the development any loss of bird life or eggs is an incidental result of a lawful operation.

Exceptions to the provisions are also provided where wild birds are taken to nurse them back to health before releasing them back into the wild (s 4(2)(a)). The Act also covers a situation where a bird is killed as a humane gesture because it has been so seriously injured that there is no reasonable chance of its recovery. Exceptions also arise where action is necessary to preserve health or public or air safety, prevent the spread of disease, or prevent serious damage to agricultural stock or crops (see below).

The WCA 1981 makes some provision for restrictions on sale of wild birds and for registering some captive birds. Under section 6 the sale, offer or exposure for sale, possession or transportation for sale of any live wild bird other than a bird listed in Part I of Schedule 3 to the Act is an offence. So is the sale of a wild bird's egg or part of such an egg or publishing an advertisement for buying or selling them.

## Birds in which trade is permitted

Birds listed in Part I of Schedule 3 to the Act are those birds in which trade is permitted provided the bird is alive, ringed and bred in captivity. The sale of Schedule 3 birds is governed by the Wildlife and Countryside (Ringing of Certain Birds) Regulations 1982. Section 27 of WCA 1981 provides that a bird shall not be treated as bred in captivity unless its parents were lawfully in captivity when the egg was laid. Any such bird must be ringed or marked and the bird keeper registered in accordance with the Wildlife and Countryside (Registration and Ringing of Certain Captive Birds) Regulations 1982 made by the Secretary of State.

Section 7 of the Act deals with the registration of birds kept in captivity. Those birds that it is necessary to register are named in Schedule 4 to the Act; they mostly consist of birds of prey. Regulations made under section 6(2), the Wildlife and Countryside (Registration to Sell, etc Certain Dead Wild Birds) Regulations 1982 make provision for registering persons who sell or have in their possession for sale dead wild birds. They also provide that no person shall be registered to keep a Schedule 4 bird if he or she has been convicted under WCA 1981. Section 7(3)(a) provides for an offence if a bird listed in Schedule 4 is kept by a person within five years of a conviction for an offence subject to a special penalty (*i.e.* an offence under section 1, 3, 5 or 8). It also provides at section 7(3)(b) that within three years of conviction for any other offence under Part I of the Act, so far as it relates to the protection of birds or offences involving their ill treatment, keeping a bird included in Schedule 4 will be an offence. The WCA 1981 stipulates certain requirements for the protection of captive birds in section 8, which provides that the size of any cage which houses a captive bird must be sufficient to allow the bird to stretch its wings freely.

## Licences to take or kill wild birds

Licences may be issued in certain circumstances to permit taking or killing wild birds. The circumstances in which licences are granted are restricted under the Act to those listed in section 16. Such circumstances include preserving public health or public or air safety, preventing the spread of disease, and preventing serious damage to livestock, foodstuffs for livestock, crops, vegetables, fruit, growing timber, fisheries or inland waters. Any licence will specify the species of wild bird and the circumstances in which and conditions subject to which the action permitted by the licence may be taken.

## 6.2 Wild animals

Part I of WCA 1981 also deals with the protection of wild animals, in so far as they are protected by English law. It should be remembered that the UK is a party to various international treaties that deal with the protection of certain endangered species of animal and that in some instances obligations under the provisions of these international treaties may arise.

### Offences relating to wild animals

The WCA 1981 provides in section 9(1) that it is an offence to intentionally kill, injure or take any wild animal listed in Schedule 5 to the Act. The Schedule includes bats, reptiles and amphibians and certain rare mammals, fish and butterflies. The Schedule is reviewed every five years and the Secretary of State has power under section 21 to add species to or remove them from the Schedule. It is also an offence to be in possession or control of any wild animal listed in Schedule 5, whether that animal is living or dead, and to possess anything derived from such an animal.

Section 9(4) makes it an offence for any person to damage, destroy or obstruct access to any structure or place that an animal listed in Schedule 5 uses for shelter or protection. It is also an offence under section 9(4)(b) to disturb any such animal while it is occupying such a place or structure. This provision is particularly significant for protection of creatures such as bats roosting in attics. Section 10(5) of WCA 1981 specifically provides that in the case of bats roosting in a domestic dwelling house, English Nature must be notified of any proposed action or operation. English Nature must then be given a reasonable time to advise on whether that operation should be carried out and, if so, how. In the case of other protected animals, any works intended to be carried out may require a licence under section 16. A licence will only be issued in certain specified circumstances, such as to preserve public safety or prevent the spread of disease. Any licence will specify the area within and the methods by which the wild animal may be killed.

Further offences arise under WCA 1981 in relation to selling or exposing for sale or having possession of, or transporting for the purposes of sale, any wild animal listed in Schedule 5. The offence is committed whether the animal is alive or dead and in relation to anything derived from such an animal. As with wild birds, it is an offence to publish or cause to be published any advertisement likely to be understood to convey an intention to buy or sell any live or dead animal or something derived from it. Any animal listed in Schedule 5 is presumed to be wild unless the contrary is proved.

Defences are provided where actions were in pursuance of:

(1) a requirement of the Ministry of Agriculture, Fisheries and Food (MAFF);
(2) a requirement of the Secretary of State under section 98 of the Agriculture Act 1947 (which gives the Secretary of State power, to prevent damage to crops, to serve a notice on a landowner requiring steps to be taken); or
(3) an order made under the Animal Health Act 1981 (which permits an order to be made to prevent the spread of disease or for the welfare or export of horses and animals).

There are also provisions to take account of situations where a wild animal is taken after injury. If it is taken with the intention of nursing the animal back to health for release back into the wild (s 10(3)(a)) or is killed as a humane act after injury from which there was no reasonable chance of recovery (s 10(3)(b)), no offence will occur. Again, a defence is provided where it can be shown that the act, unlawful under section 9, occurred as the incidental result of a lawful operation and could not reasonably be avoided (s 10(3)). However, section 10(5) provides that a person shall not be entitled to rely on this defence in relation to a bat, in which case there is an obligation to notify the English Nature office for the area in which the house is situated of the proposed operation. There is then an obligation to allow English Nature a reasonable time to advise whether the operation should be carried out and, if so, the method to be used.

Under section 10(4) an "authorised person" will not be guilty of an offence if he or she shows that the action was necessary to prevent serious damage to livestock, foodstuff for livestock, crops, vegetables, fruit, growing timber or any other form of property. This defence is available only to the extent that a licence must be applied for as reasonably practicable after it becomes apparent that such action is necessary. "Authorised person" is defined in section 27(1) to include the owner or occupier or a person authorised by him or her.

## Prohibition on certain methods of killing or taking

Section 11 of WCA 1981 prohibits certain methods of killing or taking wild animals. In this provision a "wild animal" is defined as any animal which is or (before it was killed or taken) was living wild. The section provides that it is an offence to:

(1) set in position any self-locking snare placed so as to cause bodily injury to any wild animal coming into contact with it;
(2) use to kill or take any wild animal any self-locking snare, bow or crossbow or explosive;
(3) use as a decoy any live mammal or bird; or
(4) knowingly cause or permit to be done an act mentioned above.

The methods of taking or killing a wild animal included in Schedule 6 to the Act are more extensive. For such an animal it is also an offence to set in position, with the intent of causing bodily injury to the animal, any trap or snare, electrical device for killing or stunning or poisonous, poisoned or stupefying substance. The section also lists the use of any automatic or semi-automatic weapon, device for illuminating a target or sighting device for night shooting, form of artificial light or mirror or other dazzling device or smoke or gas. The use of a sound recording and of any mechanically propelled vehicle in immediate pursuit of the wild animal is listed. It is also an offence to knowingly cause or permit any of these methods to be used.

The Secretary of State has general power to amend the methods of taking and killing referred to in the Act to comply with an international obligation. For an offence under section 11(2)(f) in relation to an animal included in Schedule 6, a specific defence is available under section 16 to show that the article in question (some form of snare trap or poison) was set in position to kill or take, in the interests of public health, agriculture, forestry, fisheries or nature conservation, any wild animal which could be lawfully killed or taken by those means. The defendant must also show that all reasonable precautions were taken to prevent injury to animals included in Schedule 6.

If a court convicts a person of any of these offences it may order forfeiture under section 21(6) of the animal itself or of any vehicle, animal, weapon or thing used to commit the offence.

### Conservation (Natural Habitats, etc) Regulations 1994

The 1994 Regulations supplement WCA 1981 in relation to "European protected species", and implement the Habitats Directive without amending the existing primary UK legislation. The species of wild animal to which the Regulations apply are listed in Schedule 2 to the Regulations and include bats, great crested newts, the common otter and the natterjack toad, all of which are already listed in Schedule 5 to WCA 1981. The offences under the Regulations are wider than those already provided under WCA 1981, but otherwise they are similar to provisions already contained in the WCA 1981. The Regulations provide similar defences and a list of prohibited methods of taking and killing which is the same in substance to that in WCA 1981, but use slightly different wording. The Regulations also provide for issuing licences in certain circumstances.

Regulation 39 provides that it is an offence to:

(1) deliberately capture or kill a wild animal of a European protected species;
(2) deliberately disturb any such animal;
(3) deliberately take or destroy any such animal's eggs; or
(4) damage or destroy such an animal's breeding site or resting place.

It is also an offence to keep, transport or sell or exchange, or offer for sale or exchange, any live or dead wild animal of a European protected species, or any part of or anything derived from any such animal. The Regulations state that all the offences apply to all stages of life of the animals to which they apply.

### Badgers

The legislation protecting badgers is consolidated in the Protection of Badgers Act 1992. The legislation reverses the burden of proof in respect of several offences so that the defendant is assumed to be committing the offence with which he or she is charged unless the contrary is shown.

## Offences

Section 1 of the Act provides that it is an offence (except as permitted by or under the Act) to wilfully or attempt to kill, injure or take a badger. It is provided that in proceedings under section 1, if there is evidence from which it could reasonably be concluded that at the time the accused was attempting to kill, injure or take a badger, he or she is presumed to have been attempting to do so unless the contrary is shown. A further offence under section 1 arises where a person has in his or her possession or under his or her control any dead badger, or any part of it or anything derived from it. Offences under section 1(1) and (3) are subject on summary conviction to up to six months' imprisonment, a fine not exceeding level 5 (£5,000) or both.

The Act provides for certain cruelty offences to apply to badgers. There is a general offence of cruelly ill-treating any badger (s 2(1)(a)), and there are offences of using badger tongs in the course of killing or taking or attempting to kill or take a badger (s 2(1)(b)) and digging for a badger (s 2(1)(c)). It is also an offence to use certain firearms for killing or taking (s 2(1)(d)). The Act reverses the burden of proof for the offence of digging for a badger. In such a case where there is evidence from which it could reasonably be concluded that the accused was digging for a badger he or she is presumed to have been doing so unless the contrary is shown. However, the burden of proof imposed on the accused is not as onerous as is placed on a prosecutor. It is sufficient for the accused to raise doubt by satisfying the court of the probability that the offence was not being committed (*R v Hudson* [1965] 1 All ER 721). Section 2 offences attract on summary conviction penalties of up to six months' imprisonment, a fine not exceeding level 5 (£5,000) or both.

Interfering with a badger sett is an offence under the Act. The offence arises where a person interferes with a badger sett with intent or through a reckless act by:

- damaging it or any part of it;
- destroying it;
- obstructing access to, or any entrance of, it;
- causing a dog to enter it; or
- disturbing a badger when it is occupying it.

*R* v *Lawrence* [1981] All ER 974 establishes that a person is reckless if he or she does an act that involves an obvious and serious risk of harmful consequences. Where there is such a risk and he or she either:

(a) fails to give any thought to the possibility of there being any such risk, or
(b) having recognised that risk nevertheless goes on to take it,

he or she will be reckless. A risk is obvious if it is so to an ordinary prudent individual rather than to the accused.

Selling a live badger or offering one for sale is an offence, as is having a live badger in one's possession or control. Marking, ringing or tagging a badger is an offence unless it is authorised by licence under the Act. Both these offences attract on summary conviction a fine not exceeding level 5 (£5,000).

*Exceptions to offences under the Act*

The Act contains a number of exceptions. By section 6 a person is not guilty of an offence if he or she takes a badger already injured to tend it, or kills a badly injured badger as an act of mercy. A similar defence to that appearing in the WCA 1981 in relation to birds also appears in this Act, in that no offence is committed by reason of unavoidably killing or injuring a badger as an incidental result of a lawful action. However, interference with a badger sett is not lawful unless a licence is obtained to do so under section 10. In this respect the general defence does not extend to actions carried out in pursuance of planning permission unless the developer carrying out that permission has also obtained a licence. The Act specifically provides that a licence may be granted to interfere with a badger sett for any development under section 55(1) of TCPA 1990. The presence of a badger sett on a development site is therefore at least a temporary bar to development. To avoid the commission of an offence, a separate licence in addition to planning permission must be obtained from English Nature.

Sections 7 and 8 provide an exception for the offences of taking, injuring or killing badgers and for interfering with a badger sett if action is necessary to prevent serious damage to land, crops, poultry or any other form of property. If it appears that the action is likely, an application for a licence should be submitted, according to the Act, "as soon as reasonably practicable". If it is not, the defence will not apply. The defence of showing that actions were the incidental results of a lawful operation and could not reasonably have been avoided is provided for the offences of damaging a badger sett, obstructing access to or the entrance of it and disturbing a badger occupying it. There are also exceptions for situations where a recognised fox-hunt is taking place with hounds. In this situation the entrances to a sett may be interfered with temporarily by obstructing them with, for example, straw, hay or loose soil. No digging into the tops or sides of the entrance is permitted and there is an obligation to remove such materials from the sett entrance the day after the hunt has taken place. On the question of interference with a badger sett, in *Lovett* v *Bussey* [1998] *The Times*, 24 April the master of a hunt stopped up a badger sett with lumps of clay earth which had not been broken up. The court held that such material could not be within the expression "loose soil" in section 8(5)(a). Rose LJ said that where a clay-based local soil was used to stop up a sett it had to be sufficiently broken up before being placed at the entrance so that it did not form a compact structure.

## Using a dog in commission of offence

The court has additional powers where a dog has been used for badger baiting. If any dog has been used in or is present at the commission of an offence and the offender is convicted, the court may order, in addition to or in substitution for any other punishment, the dog's destruction. It may also ban the offender from keeping a dog for such period as it thinks fit. Custody of a dog in contravention of a court order is an offence. The court also has power where a person is convicted of an offence under the Act to order forfeiture of any badger or badger skin and of any other weapon or article used in the commission of the offence.

Under section 10 a licence may be granted, subject to any conditions which may be contained in it:

(1) for scientific or educational purposes or for the conservation of badgers:
   (a) to kill or take, within an area specified in the licence, or sell or have in an individual's possession any number of badgers; or
   (b) to interfere with any badger sett;
(2) to take or sell badgers to any zoological gardens or a collection specified in the licence;
(3) to take badgers within a specified area for ringing or marking, or to attach to them any ring or tag;

(4) to interfere with a badger sett for development as defined in section 55(1) of TCPA 1990;

(5) to interfere with a badger sett to preserve, or for archaeological investigation of, a monument scheduled under section 1 of the Ancient Monuments and Archaeological Areas Act 1979; and

(6) to interfere with a badger sett in the course of investigating whether any offence has been committed or to gather evidence in connection with proceedings before any court.

The licences for such purposes are granted by English Nature. The Minister of Agriculture, Fisheries and Food also has powers to issue a licence, but only after consultation with English Nature:

(1) to kill or take badgers, or interfere with a badger sett, to prevent the spread of disease

(2) to kill or take badgers, or interfere with a badger sett, to prevent serious damage to land, crops, poultry or any other form of property;

(3) to interfere with a badger sett for any agricultural or forestry operation; and

(4) for any operation to maintain or improve any existing watercourse or drainage works or construct new works.

## 6.3 **Wild plants**

Section 13 of WCA 1981 provides that it is an offence for any person who is not "authorised" within the meaning of the Act to intentionally uproot any wild plant. An authorised person includes the landowner or occupier or any person authorised by the landowner. In relation to wild plants listed in Schedule 8 to WCA 1981, an offence occurs where any such plant is picked, uprooted or destroyed.

The provisions are similar to those relating to wild birds and animals for sale, possession or transportation of any plant, alive or dead, or anything derived from such a plant if it is included in Schedule 8. It is also an offence for a person to publish any advertisement likely to be understood as conveying that he or she buys or sells, or intends to buy or sell, any of those things. The defence common to wild birds and animals also appears in relation to wild plants. Section 13(3) provides that a person will not be guilty of an offence if he or she can show it was an incidental result of a lawful operation and could not reasonably have been avoided.

The Conservation (Natural Habitats, etc) Regulations 1994 provide for similar but wider offences in relation to plants that are "European protected species". There are only nine such species considered rare enough to be included in Schedule 4 to the Regulations. In respect of these plants it is an offence to collect or cut the plant, as well as to pick, uproot or destroy it. A plant is presumed to be wild unless the contrary is shown.

## 6.4 **Hedgerows**

The Hedgerow Regulations 1997 were brought into force from June 1997. They were intended to bring within planning control the removal of hedgerows. These had been removed or destroyed on a large scale because of the increasing mechanisation of British agriculture since the 1950s and fell between the controls applicable to tree felling and the normal planning restraints. The Hedgerow Regulations were made under section 97 of the Environment Act 1995 and prohibit the removal of hedgerows that meet specified criteria unless certain procedural steps are carried out.

### Application of the Regulations

The Regulations apply to any hedgerow growing in or adjacent to any common land, protected land, or land used for agriculture, forestry or breeding or keeping horses, ponies or donkeys if it has:

(1) a continuous length of or exceeding 20 metres; or
(2) a continuous length of less than 20 metres and, at each end, meets (whether by intersection or junction) another hedgerow.

Protected land is defined in the Regulations as land:

(a) managed as a nature reserve under section 21 of NPACA 1949 (a local authority nature reserve); or
(b) in relation to which a notification under section 28 of WCA 1981 is in force (an SSSI).

The Regulations set out criteria to assist the local authority in assessing whether a hedgerow falls within the Regulations by providing that a hedgerow which meets (by intersection or junction) another is to be treated as ending at the point of the intersection or junction. The Regulations also provide that for the purposes of ascertaining the length of any hedgerow, any gap resulting from a contravention of the Regulations or of less than 20 metres is treated as part of the hedgerow.

**Removal of protected hedgerows**

Hedgerows that come within the protections may not be removed under the Regulations unless the owner of land on which the hedgerow is situated has given notice to the local authority of his or her intention to remove it. The form of the notice is prescribed in Schedule 4 to the Regulations (reproduced at Appendix E) and must be accompanied by a plan and, where available, evidence that the hedgerow was planted less than 30 years ago. Once the hedgerow removal notice has been given, the hedgerow may be removed in two circumstances only: first, if the LPA has given written notice stating that the work to remove it may be carried out; or secondly, if 42 days have expired from receipt of the removal notice by the LPA without the LPA serving a hedgerow retention notice.

Where the removal of the hedgerow is proposed by a relevant utility operator, permitted development rights do not extend to negate the need for notice. Where the removal of a hedge from land that a utility operator does not own is proposed, the Regulations specifically provide that the provisions requiring notice to be given to the LPA continue to apply. Regulation 5(10) states that in such a situation references in the Regulations to the "owner" will read as references to the utility operator.

Any removal of a hedgerow must be carried out in accordance with the proposal outlined in the hedgerow removal notice within two years of the date of its service. The LPA, on receipt of a hedgerow removal notice, is obliged to consult any parish council for the area. It must do this before the 42-day period expires, or before it gives written authorisation that the hedgerow may be removed, or it serves a hedgerow retention notice.

**Hedgerow retention notices**

The LPA is not permitted by virtue of regulation 5(5) to give a hedgerow retention notice unless a hedgerow meets the definition of "important hedgerow" given in the Regulations. However, the LPA must give a hedgerow retention notice for an important hedgerow unless it is satisfied, having regard in particular to the reasons given for its proposed removal in the removal notice, that there are circumstances which justify its removal.

What then constitutes an "important hedgerow"? Regulation 4 states that a hedgerow is "important" if it or a stretch of it has existed for 30 years or more and satisfies one of the detailed criteria listed in Part II of Schedule 1 to the Regulations (reproduced at Appendix G). They seek to classify by archaeological and historical measures of importance and wildlife and landscape measures of importance. Included in the definition of "important hedgerow" is one that marks the boundary or part of the boundary of at least one historic (pre-1850) parish or township. Also defined as "important" is a hedgerow that incorporates an archaeological feature that is in the schedule of ancient monuments compiled by the Secretary of State under the Ancient Monuments and Archaeological Areas Act 1979. Hedgerows are also "important" where they have existed for 30 years or more and contain certain species of wildlife or certain woody species. A specimen hedgerow retention notice, which gives reasons for the hedgerow being designated as important, appears at Appendix F.

If the LPA serves a hedgerow retention notice it must specify each criterion of those listed in Schedule 1 that apply to the hedgerow as its reasons for doing so. The LPA is at liberty to withdraw the retention notice at any time, but while the notice is in force removal of the hedgerow is prohibited. A person who intentionally or recklessly removes, or causes or permits another person to remove, a hedgerow in contravention of the Regulations is guilty of an offence, triable either way with penalties of a fine up to the statutory maximum (£5,000) on summary conviction and an unlimited fine on indictment. What is important is that the courts are obliged in considering the level of any fine to have regard to any financial benefit that has accrued or appears likely to accrue to the defendant in consequence of the offence.

**Replacement of hedgerows**

There are useful powers in the Regulations to require hedgerows to be replanted in some circumstances. This arises where a hedgerow has been removed in contravention of the Regulations and can be used whether or not proceedings are taken to secure a criminal conviction.

The LPA gives notice to the owner or utility operator of the requirement to replant and specifies the species and position of the shrubs and/or trees to be planted and the period within which planting is to be carried out. For the purposes of administering the requirement, the Regulations apply provisions of the TCPA 1990 relating to tree preservation. Section 209 of TCPA 1990 permits an LPA to enter land and carry out the replanting it required under a formal notice issued in relation to trees subject to a tree preservation order. This power is applied to hedgerows by regulation 8. It means that the LPA may enter land, plant the replacement hedgerow it requires and recover the cost of doing so from the landowner, if the owner on whom it has served the hedgerow replacement notice fails to do so. Any obstruction of a person acting to exercise this power is an offence liable on summary conviction to a fine up to level 3 (£1,000). Once replanted, for a 30-year period from completion of the planting the hedgerow is protected as an "important" hedgerow.

## Exception to the Regulations

There are a number of exceptions to the Hedgerow Regulations. These are contained in regulation 6, which states that the removal of a hedgerow to which the Regulations apply is permitted if it is required for:

(1) making a new opening to substitute an existing opening which gives access to land (but if this exception is used an obligation arises under regulation 6(2) to fill the existing opening by planting a hedge within eight months of making the new opening);
(2) obtaining temporary access to give assistance in an emergency;
(3) obtaining access to land where another means of access is not available or is available only at disproportionate cost;
(4) national defence;
(5) carrying out development for which planning permission has been granted (but not deemed permission under the General Permitted Development Order 1995);
(6) carrying out work for flood defence or land drainage under the Land Drainage Act 1991, the Water Resources Act 1991 or the Environment Act 1995;
(7) preventing the spread, or ensuring the eradication, of:
    (a) any plant pest, within the meaning of the Plant Health (Great Britain) Order 1993, which prohibits the import into Great Britain

of any plant pest not normally present in the country and which is likely to be injurious to native plants; and

(b) any tree pest, within the meaning of the Plant Health (Forestry) (Great Britain) Order 1993, which prohibits the import of any tree pest in a similar fashion to (a) above;

(8) the Secretary of State to carry out his or her functions in respect of any highway for which he or she is the highway authority;

(9) carrying out any felling, lopping or cutting back required or permitted as a consequence of any notice given or order made under the Electricity Act 1989 (felling, lopping or cutting back to prevent obstruction of or interference with electric lines and plant or to prevent danger); or

(10) the proper management of the hedgerow.

These exceptions are only supplemented for an owner by his or her right to appeal against the imposition of a hedgerow retention notice or a notice requiring him or her to plant a replacement hedgerow. An appeal lies to the Secretary of State within 28 days of the service of the notice (reg 9). The notice must state the grounds of appeal and must be served on the LPA responsible for the service of the hedgerow retention notice or the notice requiring planting of a replacement hedgerow. The Secretary of State must before determining any appeal afford an opportunity for representations to be made either by local inquiry or hearing before an inspector appointed by him or her, or by means of written representations.

In determining any appeal, the Secretary of State may allow or dismiss the appeal, either in whole or in part, and may give any directions necessary to give effect to his or her determination. He or she is obliged to notify the LPA and appellant of his or her determination.

Any party that serves a hedgerow removal notice should be aware that the LPA is obliged to keep a public register of all notices served and of any hedgerow retention notice issued by it. The register also contains copies of notifications to it of determinations by the Secretary of State on any appeal against the issue of a retention notice. The register is available for public inspection at all reasonable hours. There is also power in the Regulations for any person authorised in writing by the LPA to enter any land to survey it. This may be in connection with a hedgerow removal notice received by the LPA, to ascertain whether an offence has been committed or to determine whether a notice should be served requiring the planting of a replacement hedgerow under regulation 8. Obstruction of the right of entry is in itself an offence liable on summary conviction to a fine not exceeding level 3 (£1,000).

**Key points**

*Wild birds*

- It is an offence to kill, injure or take any wild bird, destroy any bird's nest or an egg of a wild bird.
- Birds listed in Schedule 1 to WCA 1981 are presumed to be wild unless it is proved otherwise. Schedule 2 contains a list of species of wildfowl bird which it is permitted to kill or take outside the closed season. Offences under WCA 1981 prohibit certain methods of killing or taking wild birds, including game. Killing or taking species of pest bird listed in Part II of Schedule 2 falls outside of the WCA 1981 protections.
- Bird sanctuaries may be designated by order under section 3 of WCA 1981.
- There are exceptions to offences including acts incidental to a lawful operation and which cannot reasonably be avoided.
- The sale, offer for sale, possession or transportation of any wild bird other than those listed in Part I of Schedule 3 is an offence. Those listed in Part I are those in which trade is permitted if the bird is ringed and bred in captivity.
- Licences may be issued in certain circumstances to permit the killing or taking of wild birds.

*Wild animals*

- It is an offence to intentionally kill, injure or take any wild animal or be in possession or control of any wild animal (alive or dead) listed in Schedule 5 to WCA 1981.
- It is an offence for any person to damage, destroy or obstruct access to any structure or place that a Schedule 5 animal uses for shelter or protection. Further offences arise for selling, exposing for sale or having possession of, or transporting for the purposes of sale, any such wild animal. Any animal so listed is presumed to be wild unless it can be proved otherwise.
- There are exceptions to offences including acts incidental to a lawful operation which cannot reasonably be avoided.
- Section 11 of WCA 1981 prohibits certain methods of killing or taking wild animals.
- It is an offence to wilfully or attempt to kill, injure or take a badger. The accused is presumed to have been doing so unless

he or she can show otherwise (*i.e.* the burden of proof is reversed).

- There is a general offence under the Act of cruelly ill-treating a badger in addition to other specific offences, such as digging for a badger and interfering with a badger sett.
- There are exceptions to offences under the Act including taking a badger to tend it, or killing it as an act of mercy.
- A licence may be granted to interfere with a badger sett so as to carry out development under TCPA 1990.
- A badger sett may be interfered with temporarily where a recognised fox-hunt is taking place.
- Any dog used in the commission of an offence may in addition to other punishment be destroyed by court order, and the owner banned from keeping dogs.

## Wild plants

- It is an offence for an unauthorised person to intentionally uproot any wild plant.
- Where a plant is listed in Schedule 8 to WCA 1981 an offence occurs if it is picked, uprooted or destroyed.

## Hedgerows

- The Hedgerow Regulations 1997 were made under the Environment Act 1995 to bring within planning control the removal of hedgerows.
- There is a prohibition on removal where hedgerows meet specified criteria unless the landowner gives notice to the LPA of his or her intention to remove it. The owner is entitled to remove the hedgerow if the LPA gives notice that it may be carried out or a period of 42 days from receipt of the hedgerow removal notice has elapsed. The owner for the purposes of the Regulations includes a utility operator.
- The LPA may serve a hedgerow retention notice if the hedgerow is an "important hedgerow".
- A person who intentionally or recklessly removes, or causes or permits another person to remove, a hedgerow in contravention of the Regulations is guilty of an offence. The courts are obliged in considering the level of fine to be imposed for any offence to

have regard to any financial benefit that has accrued or is likely to accrue to the defendant in consequence of the offence.

- The LPA may require the replanting of a hedgerow removed in contravention of the Regulations.
- Exceptions include obtaining access to land or temporary access, or for carrying out development for which planning permission is granted.
- A landowner may appeal against the imposition of a hedgerow retention notice or a notice requiring the planting of a replacement hedgerow.

# Chapter 7

# Conservation and the
·  Farming Community  ·

Agriculture has traditionally been and continues to be the dominant form of land use in the British Isles. Leaving aside the built environment, agricultural practices have probably the greatest visual impact on the environment and consequently are one of the major influences on conservation. Where land in an SSSI is privately owned, it is very often land forming part of an agricultural holding and the owner or occupier of that land utilises it for agricultural purposes. The individual on the sharp end of conservation law and policy is often a farmer.

Although the wildlife habitats and natural environments that it is sought to preserve may have in many instances arisen as the direct result of agricultural practices, there has been increasing concern in recent years that the intensification of farming is harming biodiversity. Increasingly intensive methods of livestock and crop production have been responsible for the loss of wildlife habitats and landscape features. Farming practices have resulted in prairie-style arable fields designed to ease the use of large-scale farming machinery. This has sometimes caused the consequent loss of hedgerow, woodland and wild flower margins. The visual effect of these methods is the loss of a patchwork of fields in a rural landscape. Farming has also come under attack for using chemical treatments and fertilisers and polluting surface and ground water with a resulting decrease in the diversity of plant and animal life to be found on farmland.

Much of the criticism of modern farming practice has its roots in the system of grants paid to farmers which has encouraged intensification of large-scale arable and livestock farming without regard for the natural habitat and wildlife consequences of the proposed use. In recent years there have been moves to encourage farming practices that do not result in damage to the natural environment. As is the case with the majority of conservation law measures, many of these measures are voluntary, relying on the individual farming landowner to take up more environmentally friendly practices.

Most of the measures considered in this chapter may equally apply to other landowners, and not just farmers. However, the subject-matter explored here is likely to be of more interest and relevance to the farming community, although many of the measures considered represent a shift in the approach to conservation generally from a "compensation for profit foregone" attitude to a more positive emphasis whereby willing individuals are paid to perform specified activities. The vehicle of a management agreement of one type or another usually regulates these activities.

## *7.1* Restrictions on land use

The various nature conservation designations and their effect on land ownership are examined in previous chapters. The particular consequences of any designation are already explained and the restrictions on use of the land in certain circumstances considered.

The occupation of SSSI designated land means that there is at least a mandatory restriction on carrying out an operation listed as a PDO for a period of four months. If the site is also subject to a designation under the Conservation (Natural Habitats, etc) Regulations 1994, planning permission will not be granted for any plan or project that will adversely affect the site's integrity. In addition, rights under the General Permitted Development Order 1995, which in the case of agricultural operations under Part VI includes excavation and engineering operations, are curtailed. If the development is likely to have a significant effect on the European site and is not directly connected with the site's management it is not permitted unless planning permission has been obtained from the LPA. If the LPA finds that the proposal will adversely affect the site's integrity, planning permission may be granted only where there are imperative reasons of overriding public interest, human health or safety considerations, or benefits of primary importance to the environment. More detailed explanations of the SSSI regime and designations under the Conservation (Natural Habitats, etc) Regulations 1994 appear in Chapters 3 and 4.

### Management agreements

What may particularly restrict the use of land is the existence of a management agreement negotiated to protect a particular feature or habitat. As land which is subject to nature conservation designations is often working agricultural land, it is very often farmers as the owners or occupiers of that land that enter into management agreements relating to it. The National Farmers Union in its public information leaflet "Environment" quotes a figure of some 1.2 million hectares of farming land subject to agreements. Individual farmers will enter into these on a voluntary basis where land is subject to an SSSI designation or one of the designations under the Conservation (Natural Habitats, etc) Regulations 1994. The restrictive arrangements of agreements run with the land and are binding on future owners. There is, however, no effective mechanism for ensuring positive obligations run with the land.

Management agreements may be concluded under the following provisions.

*Countryside Act 1968, section 15*

It is this provision that empowers English Nature to enter into a management agreement to conserve flora, fauna or geological or physiographical features on an SSSI. The agreement may be made with the owners, lessees and occupiers of any land subject to SSSI status and may extend to land adjacent to that land. This important provision was inserted as an amendment to the section by EPA 1990. It enables agreements to be concluded which prohibit damage caused by actions on neighbouring land. For example, drainage of land neighbouring an important wetland site which might have disastrous knock-on consequences for a neighbouring protected habitat. Any agreement may impose restrictions on the exercise of rights over land by persons with an interest in land capable of being bound by means of the agreement. In particular, the agreement may provide for carrying out works or operations on land. It may also make provision for payments for the cost of any works by English Nature. Section 15(4) expressly provides that English Nature may enforce restrictions contained in a management agreement as if it were the owners of a neighbouring piece of land having the benefit of a covenant. In other words, English Nature is put in the unique position of a dominant tenement having the benefit of a covenant without the usual requirement of English law that it own the neighbouring land. The legislation also provides that section 84 of the Law of Property Act 1925, which permits the discharge or modification of restrictive covenants in certain circumstances, does not apply to restrictions imposed by way of a management agreement. In this way the burden of the agreement runs with the land, ensuring that future owners of it are bound by its terms.

*National Parks & Access to Countryside Act 1949, section 16*

If the land is subject to a nature reserve designation, English Nature will use section 16 to conclude any necessary management agreement. English Nature will have control of land subject to an NNR designation, but the instrument of a management agreement may be used where other parties have occupation of or an interest in the land. Any such agreement may impose restrictions on the exercise of rights over the land by persons with an interest that can be bound by the agreement.

*Conservation (Natural Habitats, etc) Regulations 1994, regulation 16*

This regulation extends the power for management agreements to be concluded where land forms part of a "European site". A European site is one designated as an SAC or SPA; a more detailed explanation of the designation of such sites is given at pages 16-24. The regulation provides that any management agreement may provide for management of the land or doing things on the land as is considered expedient. It may also make provision for payment of costs of any necessary works and compensation payments in return for the restrictions on the land. As in section 15 of CA 1968 (see above), the agreement is enforceable as if English Nature were owners of adjacent land holding the benefit of a covenant.

**Measures imposed through land law system**

In addition to the covenants contained in management agreements, which may be enforced by English Nature as if it were the owners of adjoining land, land may be subject to covenants that have the direct or indirect result of furthering conservation. These may be restrictions on the land imposed regardless of the land's status. In other words, the land does not have to be an SSSI or other recognised nature conservation site for ordinary land law restrictions to be imposed when its ownership is severed. The purpose of restrictive covenants is to impose restrictions for the direct benefit of the neighbouring landowner. They may also have the indirect result of furthering conservation, for example by restricting building or certain activities on the land.

The scope and extent of particular covenants may in some circumstances restrict the use of the land for all time and ensure that activities damaging to habitat and wildlife cannot take place. In years past the use of available land law restrictions has been an important component in furthering nature conservation. These mechanisms are still used today to limit use of land. Bodies such as the National Trust are examples of organisations the statutory purpose of which is to preserve historical monuments and buildings, land of scientific interest and natural beauty for the benefit of future generations. They incorporate into their leases with tenants certain restrictive covenants which have the effect of furthering nature conservation. The importance of such covenants as a restriction on a landowner or occupier in certain circumstances should not be underestimated.

A detailed examination of the law of covenants is beyond the scope of this text. However, the possibility of such devices constituting a restriction of assistance to conservation should be borne in mind.

## 7.2 Incentive measures and schemes for conservation in agriculture

### Environmentally sensitive areas

The Minister of Agriculture, Fisheries and Food designates environmentally sensitive areas (ESAs) under the Agriculture Act 1986. The Act provides at section 17 that in discharging any functions connected with agriculture in relation to land the Minister is obliged to have regard to and endeavour to achieve a reasonable balance between:

(1) promoting and maintaining a stable and efficient agricultural industry;
(2) the economic and social interests of rural areas;
(3) the conservation and enhancement of the countryside's natural beauty and amenity (including its flora, fauna and geological and physiographical features) and of any features of archaeological interest there; and
(4) promoting the enjoyment of the countryside by the public.

The procedure for designation is set out in section 18 of the 1986 Act. If it appears to the Minister that it is particularly desirable to

(a) conserve and enhance an area's natural beauty,
(b) conserve an area's flora, fauna or geological or physiographical features, or
(c) protect an area's buildings or other objects of archaeological, architectural or historic interest,

and that the maintenance or adoption of particular agricultural methods is likely to facilitate such conservation, enhancement or protection, he or she may designate an ESA. Any designation must be with the Treasury's consent and after consultation with the Countryside Agency and English Nature on the area to be included in any order and the features for which conservation, enhancement or protection is desirable.

The Act empowers the MAFF to conclude personal contracts with farmers or any person who agrees to participate in the scheme having an interest in agricultural land in the area of the order. An agreement concluded under the provisions of the Act is a personal contract with the owner for the time being of the land. The burden of any agreement runs with the land by virtue of section 18(7), which provides that unless the agreement specifically provides otherwise it is binding on persons deriving title from the owner who entered into it. In consideration of payments made by MAFF the land is managed in accordance with the agreement.

Any agreement will require farmers to undertake specified farming practices appropriate to each designated ESA in consideration of the payments made. These are payable annually for each hectare subject to the agreement. The contract usually lasts for 10 years. The agreements are of varying degrees of stringency and compensation is paid according to the level of management required under the agreement. More stringent requirements will attract greater compensation payments, and areas where conservation is considered a greater priority will also attract larger payments.

The scheme for ESA conservation is open to any farmer in a designated ESA who chooses to participate. Many ESAs are designated in areas already subject to other UK designations such as national parks and areas of outstanding natural beauty and have proved an effective way of furthering conservation by maintaining and adopting particular agricultural methods in many of these particularly important areas.

### Countryside Stewardship Scheme

Powers are granted under section 4 of CA 1968 for the Countryside

Agency (after consultation with interested local authorities and other bodies which have an interest) to carry out or promote the carrying out of experimental schemes. These must be designed to facilitate the enjoyment of the countryside, or to conserve or enhance its natural beauty or amenity. It was on this experimental basis that the Countryside Stewardship Scheme (CSS) was originally introduced between 1990 and 1996. After its initial trial under powers conferred by section 4, the scheme has been continued by the MAFF. The scheme is set out in the Countryside Stewardship Regulations 1998.

The CSS involves the payment of grant to landowners (not necessarily farmers) who undertake measures to improve the beauty and diversity of the countryside. It operates in all areas in England that are not designated ESAs and may apply to sites that are not subject to a management agreement under another designation. It can be applied for in areas subject to a nature conservation designation such as an SSSI with English Nature's consent provided no other management agreement is in force in respect of the land. The CSS aims to encourage the adaptation of land management to enrich countryside features and extend access and enjoyment for the public. It is granted only to landowners or occupiers able to exercise control of the land for the length of the agreement concluded for it, which is usually 10 years. The scheme is aimed at management of normal agricultural operations so that usually works agreed under it will not be operations that require planning permission from the LPA. However, some proposed works may require consents; examples are where works are planned to a scheduled monument which requires Scheduled Monument Consent, or works which may affect watercourses which may require consent from the Environment Agency or an internal drainage board.

The CSS's objectives are to:

- sustain the beauty and diversity of the landscape
- improve and extend wildlife habitats
- conserve archaeological sites and historic features
- improve opportunities for countryside enjoyment
- restore neglected land or features
- create new habitats and landscapes.

The scheme applies to specific types of landscape and landscape features. These include chalk and limestone grassland, lowland heath, waterside land, coastal land, upland, old meadows and pasture, historic features such as orchards and parklands, field boundaries such as stonewalls, hedgerows and ditches, arable field margins, community forests and urban fringes and new access.

Each grant application is individually assessed; as funds are limited to those schemes offering the best diversity which meet the CSS's objectives, not all applications receive grant aid. Payments by way of grant depend on the proposals of each individual landowner or occupier for management of the land. Certain items of work attract a fixed payment: for example, the erection of a kissing gate (which must not be a gate that the owner is obliged to maintain because the path in question is a public right of way) results at the time of writing in a grant payment of £130.

### Terms of agreement under CSS

Agreements for the scheme contain a set of standard conditions which must be fulfilled. Individual schedules detail the works proposed or management practices required for each individual proposal. A map of the land in question is appended to each agreement, which also sets out the payments due under it.

Agreements usually run for 10 years. In some cases where the type of works proposed demands it, this extends to 20 years. Each agreement commences on 1 October in any year. Early withdrawal from the agreement is a breach of it and sanctions such as withholding payments due may be imposed. Dates for completing works are timetabled in the agreement; it also constitutes a breach of the agreement if works required to take place in any year are not carried out. Claims must be submitted for payment of grant each year. Payments are not made automatically and the agreement holder is required to submit a claim form to the MAFF within the time frame provided for in the agreement.

Other activities carried out on the land by the owner or occupier must not conflict with the CSS's objectives. If it is intended to carry out any other activity, the MAFF's consent must be obtained. The agreement also contains clauses that require the landowner or occupier to conserve other features of conservation and amenity interest on his or her landholding even if these are outside the area of land subject to CSS grant. Any shooting or hunting activities, or activities carried out under permitted development rights, may also be restricted if they conflict with the scheme objectives.

A general obligation to comply with all relevant legislation is imposed under the agreement. It is specifically stated in guidance issued by the MAFF that any individual who joins the scheme who is found guilty of an offence related to public rights of way may have his or her agreement terminated. The land is inspected from time to time to monitor the works and land management arrangements under the agreement and there may be obligations to keep records of management activities. These records may also be subject to inspection.

There are also usually certain standard requirements in any agreement. These include an obligation to manage grazing to avoid damage, not to disturb the land by ploughing or other cultivation unless this is provided for in the agreement, to minimise disturbance to wildlife and to limit herbicide and pesticide application to spot treatment. Grazing livestock numbers may also need to be adjusted.

In certain circumstances the submission of a claim for CSS grant needs to be supported by a management plan or an Upland Survey. Some costs for professional advice in connection with preparing the plan or survey may be reclaimed through the CSS if the application is accepted.

## Wildlife enhancement scheme

This scheme is run by English Nature and provides financial incentives for owners and occupiers of SSSIs to carry out management practices that are sympathetic to wildlife. The scheme cannot be applied for where land is subject to an existing SSSI management agreement. Unlike the CSS, this scheme does not aim to further public access to the land, as creation of new or improved wildlife habitat may not necessarily co-exist comfortably with extended public access. The scheme offers two types of payment in return for positive management to enhance wildlife: one is an annual payment for the term of the agreement for managing the site to sustain its wildlife interest; the other is a fixed cost payment for particular works carried out on the land, in a similar way to fixed payments under the CSS. Payments are made under short-term agreements, usually lasting for a period of five years.

## Key points

- There are increasing efforts to encourage farming practices that do not damage the natural environment.
- Many conservation measures are voluntary, relying on the

individual landowner to take up more environmentally friendly practices.

- Management agreements may be negotiated to protect a particular feature or habitat and individual landowners enter into these on a voluntary basis where land is subject to an SSSI or an international designation under the Habitats Regulations 1994.
- Land may be subject to covenants that have the direct or indirect result of furthering conservation imposed regardless of the status of the land when its ownership is severed.
- Environmentally sensitive areas are designated under the Agriculture Act 1986.
- Personal contracts may be concluded with persons having an interest in agricultural land and in consideration of payments made by the MAFF the land is managed in accordance with the agreement.
- The Countryside Stewardship Scheme involves the payment of grant to landowners that undertake measures to improve the beauty and diversity of the countryside. It aims to encourage the adaptation of land management to enrich countryside features and extend access and enjoyment for the public. Agreements contain a set of standard conditions with individual schedules detailing the works or proposed management practices. Land is inspected to monitor compliance with the agreement.
- The wildlife enhancement scheme provides financial incentives for owners and occupiers of SSSI land to carry out management practices that are sympathetic to wildlife.

## Chapter 8

# Local Authorities and
# ▪     Conservation     ▪

In England and Wales it is the local authority that routinely has responsibility for protecting important nature conservation sites and furthering nature conservation objectives. This is usually an element of the authority's functions as the LPA. Local authorities are invaluable for conservation by incorporating into the planning process the necessary considerations to ensure that nature conservation is taken into account in the decision-making process. They also play a positive role in furthering nature conservation locally by designating sites as local nature reserves. They may have ownership of land that is of local conservation importance and this ownership often ensures the management of it in a manner that enhances its conservation interest. Such ownership may also ensure protection from development pressures.

This chapter considers the involvement of local authorities in nature conservation and how they help to further conservation objectives.

## 8.1 Conservation and the local planning authority

As is evident from previous chapters in consideration of the nature conservation regime, the specific nature conservation designations and the subsequent protections afforded to sites are very often inadequate to fully protect a site. In situations where planning permission is required for a development, what may ensure that development does not take place to the detriment of nature conservation is the planning system, administered through the LPA.

A detailed discussion of planning law is outside the scope of this work, but there are many specialist texts on planning law. Instead, this chapter outlines the framework within which local authorities operate and considers the policy guidance.

Where development is proposed, an understanding of the planning system in relation to nature conservation is extremely important. The policy framework needs to be appreciated not only by those who seek increased protections for a site, but also by those who own, occupy or manage a site subject to a local or national conservation designation.

## The development plan system

In any planning decision the LPA is obliged to take into account the statutory plan so far as it is material to the application. In addition, in accordance with section 54A of TCPA 1990, where it is obliged to have regard to the local development plan policies it must make decisions in accordance with the plan unless material considerations indicate otherwise. Effectively, section 54A means that there is a presumption in favour of the development plan and any development that does not conform to it must show other "material considerations" or convincing reasons why it should not be followed and the development should be granted permission. There are always other matters to be weighed in the balance when considering whether the development plan should prevail. In particular, other policy documents such as PPGs and circulars are relevant, the results of consultations and representations need to be given due weight and any other material considerations on the facts of the particular case must be considered.

The development plan is defined in section 54 of TCPA 1990 as, outside Greater London and the metropolitan counties, the structure plan and any alterations made to it by the local authority and the local plan and any alterations made to it. The structure plan is prepared by the county planning authority and sets out general policies for future development in the area. The local plan supplements the structure plan skeleton by outlining detailed planning policy for a district council's area. The local plan policies will be in line with the structure plan guidance, which deals with certain key strategic issues such as allocation of land for housing, industrial and commercial development, highways and transport, minerals, waste disposal and green belt and conservation issues.

In metropolitan areas and Greater London, the unitary development plan and any alterations made to it are the development plan. Local plans may be revised and the weight of the policies in the plan may change with the age of the plan and other factors such as its conformity with government guidance. The LPA must take account of government guidance when preparing its local development plan. PPGs issued by the Secretary of State, although having no formal statutory force, constitute current government policy on a topic.

Conformity with development plan policies are the LPA's initial consideration in reaching any decision on an application for planning permission. In most cases, local plans contain particular policies for certain areas of the LPA's jurisdiction where landscape or other features merit particular safeguards. If, for example, a site is in a designated green belt, a presumption against development will be enshrined in the plan as well as being contrary to government policy. This will apply unless it falls into particular categories of development appropriate to the local conditions or, in accordance with government guidance contained in PPG2, very special circumstances exist to justify development. In some cases a local designation applies. For example, the site may fall within a defined special landscape area or nature conservation enhancement area designated by the plan as being of particular local importance, and so special restraints on development may apply. The extent of such an area will be illustrated in a map appended to the plan. In such designated areas proposals which may adversely affect the quality or character of the landscape are not normally permitted. The creation of new habitats and measures aimed at increasing the nature conservation value of existing areas would also be sought by the LPA in making planning decisions. Unless a proposal satisfies the constraints of a relevant policy or will satisfy it with the attachment of appropriate conditions, the presumption will be against granting permission.

### Sites subject to national nature conservation designations

Where a development is proposed within a site subject to a national designation, the LPA under Article 10 of the General Development Procedure Order 1995 must consult English Nature before taking a decision on whether to grant planning permission. If permission is granted for development, it overrides any nature conservation designation. Any representation by English Nature is a material consideration in the planning decision-making process. This means that English Nature's advice is a factor to be weighed in the balance by the LPA when making a planning decision. The representations do not, however, constitute an overriding consideration in any LPA decision. There are instances where LPAs have not acted in accordance with advice from English Nature.

In *R* v *Poole Borough Council*, *ex parte Beebee* [1991] JPL 643, for example, the site's status was one of the issues examined. The issue arose in relation to submissions put to the court that not all-relevant considerations had been taken into account in the council's decision to issue planning permission for the site. Canford Heath contained a designated SSSI and the council had been notified by the then NCC that it intended to extend this area so that it would include the site of the planning permission. The council had objected to the intended extension, but under section 28 of WCA 1981 the site was protected while the NCC considered the objections lodged against the designation. It was accepted as common ground that the subject site was part of an SSSI and that this was a relevant consideration for the council. The council's decision to grant planning permission for the site was challenged on the ground, among others, that the council had not taken into account a relevant consideration - that the site was part of an SSSI. The challenge was unsuccessful. Schiemann J found that the LPA had in fact taken into account the substance of what it was required to take into account. He was persuaded that the LPA's approach could be faulted, but that the decision to grant planning permission should not be quashed because, in this case, the errors made no difference to the result.

In fact, the Secretary of State took the step of revoking the grant of permission in exercise of his powers under section 100 of TCPA 1990. These powers are rarely invoked because of the necessity to pay compensation under section 107 where expenditure has been incurred by carrying out work or other loss or damage is sustained which is directly attributable to the revocation. Since *Poole Borough Council*, the strengthening of nature conservation protections under the Conservation (Natural Habitats, etc) Regulations 1994 means that any site designated an SSSI also with an international conservation designation would not suffer a similar fate unless the necessary criteria could be met in accordance with the Regulations. The test now would be whether imperative reasons of overriding public interest exist or there are human health or safety considerations or benefits of primary importance to the environment. The stricter controls and stronger government guidance mean that a situation such as that which arose at Canford Heath is unlikely to be repeated. In the event that an LPA does intend to grant planning permission against English Nature's advice, government guidance in PPG9 requires it to notify English Nature so that representations can be made for the application to be called in for determination. Unfortunately, this does not necessarily mean the protection of all sites will be championed: the inability of the department to intervene in Canford Heath resulted in the revocation of the planning permission after the event.

If the site is subject to a European designation under the 1994 Regulations, detailed guidance is given in PPG9 to LPAs on dealing with any planning application (see further below).

## Local authority enforcement powers

If development is carried out without the benefit of planning permission, the LPA may decide to take enforcement action to remedy the breach. "Development" is defined to include both operational development and material changes of use of premises. What does and does not constitute development has been subject to much argument and, despite detailed provision in the legislation, it has proved a fruitful area in the courts. Enforcement is the mechanism used to bring land back to its lawful condition or use and is used in areas of land subject to a nature conservation designation in just the same way as it would be used elsewhere. It extends to a failure to comply with conditions subject to which a planning permission has been granted.

A number of enforcement options are available to the LPA. These are considered briefly here, but reference to a detailed planning text is necessary where land is the subject of enforcement action. Enforcement action can only be taken in the case of a building or structure if not more than four years have elapsed from the breach of planning control complained of. Where a change of use is alleged, the use must not have continued for a period in excess of 10 years. In such circumstances the building or use is immune from enforcement action.

### Planning contravention notice

Where the LPA suspects a breach of planning control has occurred it may serve a planning contravention notice under section 171C of TCPA 1990 requiring the owner, occupier or other person having an interest in the land to give information about ownership or occupation or the activities being carried out on it. In fact, the information the LPA can request is limited only by the fact that it should be information properly necessary for it to investigate the alleged breach of planning control. Failure to comply with the notice is a criminal offence (s 171D).

### Enforcement notice

If a breach of planning control has occurred the LPA may take enforcement action under section 172 of TCPA 1990. The enforcement notice must be served on every owner, occupier or other person having an interest in the land. It will require the cessation of the use or operation in breach of planning control or demolition of buildings and the return of the land to its condition before the breach occurred. The notice itself contains a date on which it will become effective and if the notice is not appealed against before that date (not less than 28 days from the date of service of the notice), failure to comply with it is a criminal offence (s 179). Where an appeal against the notice is made the effect of the notice is suspended pending the outcome of the appeal unless the LPA issues a stop notice in respect of the site. PPG9 urges LPAs to issue stop notices for sites subject to a nature conservation designation where a continuing breach of planning control may result in serious harm to a site. A stop notice requires the immediate cessation of the activity even where an appeal has been entered. The grounds of appeal against an enforcement notice are set out in section 174 of TCPA 1990.

## *8.2* **Government guidance - PPGs**

When an LPA makes a planning decision it will have regard to any relevant planning policy guidance notes. Local authorities are obliged to take account of PPGs when preparing their development plans. The guidance is also a material consideration in relation to planning applications and appeals. There are three PPGs of particular relevance to nature conservation and landscape protection.

### PPG9: Nature Conservation

This PPG gives LPAs guidance on how the Government's policies for nature conservation are to be reflected in land use planning decisions. It emphasises in particular the decision-making process to be followed where a site of international importance is involved in a planning application. A site of international importance is one designated an SAC, SPA, a Ramsar site or a site proposed to be designated any of these. PPG9 states the Government's objectives for nature conservation, which the LPA is often responsible for implementing in accordance with the guidance. The Government's stated objectives are to ensure that "policies contribute to the conservation of the abundance and diversity of wildlife and its habitats, or minimise the adverse effects on wildlife where conflict of interest is unavoidable, and to meet [its] international responsibilities and obligations for nature conservation". The Government's view, detailed in the PPG, is that with careful planning and control, conservation and development can be compatible. What is clear from the guidance is that nature conservation can be a significant material consideration in determining planning applications.

PPG9 is comprehensive in its guidance. It sets out the main statutory nature conservation designations and gives a résumé of the protection that results from such designations. In particular it offers the LPA detailed guidance on dealing with planning applications in a site subject to a designation under the Conservation (Natural Habitats, etc) Regulations 1994. (A detailed consideration of the Regulations themselves appears at pp 27-40.) It also gives guidance in respect of sites subject to various international obligations to which the UK is a party. The PPG does not overlook the importance of areas of local nature conservation importance and stresses the fact that statutory and non-statutory sites, together with features which provide "wildlife corridors, links or stepping stones from one habitat to another", contribute to the diversity of the environment. The guidance states that LPAs must have regard to the relative importance of the various statutory and non-statutory designations of sites in considering the weight to be attached to nature conservation interests. To comply with PPG9 local authorities' development plans should always identify key sites of nature conservation importance and through the vehicle of the local plan should ensure the protection and enhancement of such interests.

The PPG stresses that nature conservation can be a significant material consideration in the decision-making process for planning applications. In the case of an SSSI site there is a statutory obligation on the LPA to consult English Nature on a planning application. Article 10 of the General Development Procedure Order 1995 imposes this. The LPA is directed by PPG9 not to refuse planning permission if planning conditions or obligations can be used to overcome the nature conservation objections to development at a site. What is made clear in the guidance is that development proposals in SSSI sites must be subject to special scrutiny. Proposals having an effect on an SSSI also require consultation, as may those neighbouring an SSSI where a "consultation zone" (*i.e.* an area neighbouring the site where activities may effect it) may have been determined by English Nature. If an LPA decides to grant a planning permission in an SSSI against English Nature's advice PPG9 requires the LPA to notify English Nature so that it can consider asking the Secretary of State to call in the application. A "call in" means that the Secretary of State takes the decision out of the LPA's jurisdiction for his or her own determination following an inquiry, report and recommendation by one of his or her inspectors.

At Annex C, PPG9 provides an outline of an LPA's duties to review planning permissions granted in sites classified or where consultations take place preparatory to designation as an SPA or SAC in accordance with the 1994 Regulations. It also contains guidance for LPAs where development is likely to significantly affect an SPA or SAC. The guidance makes it clear that where potential SPAs or SACs have yet to be agreed with the Commission as a matter of policy, development proposals affecting them should be considered in the same way as if such sites had already been classified or designated. The protections also extend to Ramsar sites listed under the Convention on Wetlands of International Importance. In the case of sites of international importance (SACs, SPAs or Ramsar sites), the Secretary of State usually calls in development applications likely to have significant effects on such sites for his or her own decision. Any proposal by an LPA to permit development that would adversely affect an SPA or SAC raises an obligation to notify the Secretary of State in advance of taking the decision. In this way the Secretary of State can decide whether to call in the application for his or her own decision before granting planning permission.

PPG9 gives guidance on the decision-making process where development proposals may affect an SPA or SAC. This involves consideration of whether the development is directly connected with or necessary to site management for nature conservation and whether it is likely to have a significant effect on the site. English Nature's advice is necessary for the LPA to properly consider this question. In certain circumstances a full assessment of the implications for the site may be necessary. This could correspond to a full environmental assessment exercise where the development is one not normally requiring such an assessment under the Town and Country Planning (Environmental Impact Assessment) Regulations 1999. However, English Nature's simple written opinion that no adverse effects will occur does in some circumstances suffice.

If the development is considered likely to significantly affect an SPA or SAC the proposal must be assessed having regard to the site's conservation objectives. This means the proposal must be assessed against the reasons for designation of the site. If after this consideration the proposal is found to adversely affect the site's integrity and this objection cannot be overcome by conditions, the LPA must not grant planning permission for the development unless particular defined circumstances exist. The site's integrity is defined in PPG9 as "the coherence of its ecological structure and function, across its whole area, that enables it to sustain the habitat, complex of habitats and/or the levels of populations for which it was classified". Where adverse effects on the site's integrity are anticipated the LPA is obliged to consider whether there are alternative solutions. Applicants for development should also have fully considered alternative solutions. If no alternative solution exists planning permission must not be granted unless the proposed development must be carried out for imperative reasons of overriding public importance; these can include reasons of a social and economic nature. Where a site hosts a priority species or habitat, the only circumstance where planning permission may be granted is where there are reasons of human health, public safety, or beneficial consequences of primary importance to the environment. A flowchart contained in PPG9 which illustrates the decision-making process is reproduced at Appendix C.

Where a developer proposes to exercise permitted development rights, those rights may not be available in relation to a particular site if they would result in a breach of the terms of the Habitats Directive as implemented by the 1994 Regulations. Regulations 60-63 prevent development likely to have a significant effect on a classified SPA or SAC from benefiting from permitted development rights. This is the case unless it has been decided after consultation with English Nature that the proposals will not adversely effect the site's integrity. Again, PPG9 contains a helpful flowchart to illustrate the decision-making process for both LPAs and developers, reproduced at Appendix D. If development is carried out which would usually benefit from permitted development rights but because of the significant effect on a designated site those permitted development rights do not apply, a developer will be at risk of enforcement action. The PPG provides for situations where developers are unsure of the extent of the effect of their proposals by advising that English Nature's advice be obtained on their significance prior to carrying out works.

The PPG stresses that LPAs should implement specific procedures to prevent or quickly remedy any alleged breach of planning control. In the case of a continuing breach of planning control that may result in serious harm to a site, LPAs are urged to consider serving a stop notice (see p 116 above). If the enforcement notice is appealed against on one of the grounds set out in section 174 of TCPA 1990, the activity can continue until determination of the appeal. If the appeal is dismissed the enforcement notice will come into force and will state within it a reasonable time for compliance with it.

The PPG contains an annex which deals with a much less modern piece of conservation legislation, CA 1968. The guidance stresses that local authorities have a duty under section 11 of that Act "to have regard to the desirability of conserving the natural beauty and amenity of the countryside" and that this duty should be taken seriously and "shared with the whole community". Authorities are encouraged to consider measures to further this responsibility including:

- the use of byelaws to support local nature conservation objectives;
- making tree preservation orders under planning legislation;
- creating new wildlife habitats through restoration of mineral workings and reclamation of derelict land;
- pond restoration and creation;
- entering into management agreements with owners and occupiers of land (under WCA 1981, s 39), and making loans and grants;
- managing local authority land so that account is taken of its wildlife interest, for example in the sympathetic treatment of roadside verges, open spaces and parks and in environmental improvement schemes; and
- educational activities, such as establishing nature conservation areas in school grounds and the providing information about conservation.

### PPG7: The Countryside: Environmental Quality and Economic and Social Development

This PPG is designed to give advice to local authorities on the role of the planning system in relation to the countryside. It gives guidance on special considerations in designated areas including national parks, areas of outstanding natural beauty, green belts, nature conservation sites and local countryside designations.

Planning policies and development in areas subject to statutory designations must take full account of those designations and the LPA must have regard to the specific features or qualities that justified designation of the area. Decisions in relation to the area should sustain or further the purposes of that designation.

In guidance on NPs the PPG states that the Government regards NP designation as conferring the highest status of protection as far as landscape and scenic beauty are concerned. It also reiterates the fact that the statutory purposes of NPs are to "conserve and enhance their natural beauty, wildlife and cultural heritage, and to promote opportunities for public understanding and enjoyment of their special qualities". As is enshrined in NPACA 1949 (as amended), where any conflict arises greater weight must be given by local authorities (or the relevant NPA) to conserving and enhancing an NP's natural beauty, wildlife and cultural heritage. The PPG specifically states that major development should not take place in the NP except in exceptional circumstances. Applications for any major development must be subject to the most vigorous examination and the development must be demonstrated to be in the public interest before being allowed to proceed. The NPA or local authority is advised that it "can reasonably expect a prospective developer to address the issue of the impact of the proposal on these areas and to place more explicit emphasis on the consideration of alternative options".

For AONBs, local authorities are to reflect the objective of conservation of natural beauty of the landscape in development plans and in development control. The Government expresses its approval of voluntary administration arrangements for AONBs by setting up joint advisory committees to bring together local authorities and amenity groups, farming and other interests to encourage a co-ordinated approach to management. The guidance states that in general, development control decisions in AONBs should favour conservation of the landscape, and only proven national interest and lack of alternative sites could justify any major industrial or commercial development in a designated area.

PPG7 does not modify in any way Government policy guidance on green belts. It points out that green belt policy of a presumption against inappropriate development will apply in addition to other policies outlined in PPG7 and the relevant development plan. If development does not fall within specific defined categories it is inappropriate development and will only be permitted if very special circumstances can be shown for why development should be permitted. In relation to sites of nature conservation such as SSSIs, SPAs and SACs, local authorities are referred to the detailed guidance in PPG9. Local authorities are also reminded that designations such as ESAs are important features in the local countryside and must be taken into account in countryside planning policies and development control decisions.

In relation to local countryside designations incorporated into local plans, PPG7 notes that local authorities have introduced various designations which will carry less weight in local planning decisions than national designations. Local authorities are warned that these designations may restrict acceptable development. They are advised that they should only maintain or extend local countryside designations where "there is good reason to believe that normal planning policies cannot provide the necessary protections". It is clear from the guidance that local authorities are expected to state in their development plans what it is that requires extra protections and why. On review of development plans, local authorities are expected to consider rigorously the function and justification of existing local countryside designations to ensure that they are soundly based on a formal assessment of their qualities.

## PPG2: Green Belts

This PPG explains the general presumption against inappropriate development in and the purposes of including land within a green belt. The stated purposes of green belt land includes the aim of checking the unrestricted sprawl of large, built-up areas and to assist in safeguarding the countryside from encroachment. Once land has been included in a green belt, PPG2 states that the use of the land should have a positive role to play in fulfilling the objectives of providing opportunities for access to the open countryside for the urban population and to secure nature conservation interest. Green belts are emphasised to be permanent and control over development in a green belt is strict.

There is a general presumption against inappropriate development within a green belt and LPAs should not approve development within one except in very special circumstances. As any planning application for inappropriate development will not be in accordance with the development plan, it will be classed as a departure application which, if the LPA is minded to grant permission, must be referred to the Secretary of State. He or she may decide to call in the application for his or her own decision and will attach substantial weight to the harm to the green belt when considering any planning application or appeal concerning such development.

For planning permission to be granted for development in a green belt the application must meet certain specified criteria for it to be deemed appropriate development. In all other cases the applicant must show that there are very special circumstances for the proposed development which outweighs the harm to the green belt.

## 8.3 Local authorities' roles in furthering local nature conservation

### Local nature reserves

Local authorities are given the same powers as English Nature in relation to NNRs under section 21 of NPACA 1949. This gives power to designate local nature reserves in the area of their jurisdiction. Local authorities are obliged to consult with English Nature before designation and should be satisfied that a proposed reserve has local significance.

A local authority can secure management agreements. Section 21 applies the provisions of Part III of the Act to local authorities with the substitution of local authorities for references to English Nature. It is open to a local authority to enter into agreements for establishing local nature reserves where it considers it expedient to do so in the local interest. Payments in return for owners and occupiers entering into an agreement may be made under the terms of any agreement. Local authorities may also make byelaws to protect the nature reserve.

### Ownership of land of special interest or features

Local authorities sometimes own land of special interest or take conservation enhancement measures on land in which they have an interest. In this way their role in local conservation can be important and can extend from sites which they intend to designate as local nature reserves after conservation management practices have been followed to strips of verge and hedgerow adjacent to the highway. Authorities are advised to exercise their powers under CA 1968 to manage their land to take account of its wildlife interest. This includes the sympathetic treatment of roadside verges, open spaces and parks and environmental improvement schemes.

### Access to the countryside

This subject is considered in more detail at pages 76-78. The provisions for access to the countryside are governed at present by NPACA 1949. There are proposals for amendment to the legislative framework to provide a new statutory right of access on foot for open-air recreation to specified categories of open countryside. These proposals are considered at page 13.

The NPACA 1949 provides that a local authority may make access agreements relating to open country in its area. These agreements are made with the aim of enabling the public to have access for open-air recreation to open countryside.

The procedures for making an access order are set out in Schedule 1 to NPACA 1949; where such an order is made, it must be submitted to the Secretary of State for confirmation. Compensation is payable where the value of a person's interest in land is depreciated as a consequence of the order.

If land is subject to an access order its owner is prohibited from carrying out work on the land which results in a substantial reduction of public access.

## Key points

- Local authorities incorporate into the planning process the necessary considerations to ensure that nature conservation is taken into account in the decision-making process.
- In any planning decision the LPA is obliged to take into account the statutory plan and to make decisions in accordance with it unless material considerations indicate otherwise. Development which is not in accordance with the plan should only be permitted if other material considerations outweigh the policy guidance.
- Local plans usually contain particular policies for certain areas of the planning authority's jurisdiction where landscape or other features merit particular safeguards.
- Where development is proposed on nature conservation designated land the LPA must consult English Nature before taking a decision on the application. Any representation on a planning application by English Nature is a material consideration for the local authority to take into account.
- The LPA will have regard to any relevant planning policy guidance notes in making planning decisions.
- Local authorities can designate local nature reserves. Management agreements may be concluded in respect of such nature reserves.

- Local authorities sometimes own land of special interest or take conservation enhancement measures on their own land to the benefit of nature conservation.
- Local authorities may make access agreements relating to open country to allow public access for open-air recreation.

# · Bibliography ·

## Books

Bell, Stuart, *Ball & Bell on Environmental Law* (Blackstone Press)
Birnie, P W & Boyle, A, *Basic Documents on International Law and the Environment* (Oxford University Press)
Brooman, S & Legge, Dr D, *The Law Relating to Animals* (Cavendish Publishing)
Craig, P P, *Administrative Law* (Sweet & Maxwell)
de Klemm & Shine, *Legal Measures for the Conservation of Natural Areas* (Council of Europe Publishing)
Fry, M, *A Manual of Nature Conservation Law* (Clarendon Press)
Garner, J F & Jones, B L, *Countryside Law* (Shaw & Sons)
Howarth, W & Rodgers, C P (Eds), *Agriculture Conservation and Land Use* (University of Wales Press)
Moore, Victor, *A Practical Approach to Planning Law* (Blackstone Press)
Sands, P, *Principles of International Environmental Law* (Manchester University Press)

## Articles

Harte, JDC, "Nature Conservation: The Framework for Designating Special Protection Areas for Birds" in (1995) *Journal of Environmental Law* 245
Payne, S, "Nature Conservation and Development" in [1993] *Journal of Planning and Environmental Law* 979
Purdue, M, "When a Regulation of Land becomes a Taking of Land - A Look at Two Recent Decisions of the United States Supreme Court" in [1995] *Journal of Planning and Environmental Law* 279
Rowan-Robinson, J & Ross, A, "Compensation for Environmental Protection in Britain: a Legislative Lottery" in (1995) 5(2) *Journal of Environmental Law* 245

Warren, L, "Conservation - A Secondary Environmental Consideration" (1991) 18(1) *Journal of Law and Society*

Warren, L & Murray, V, "PPG9 Nature Conservation - A New Initiative" [1995] *Journal of Planning and Environmental Law* 574

Wouter PJ Wils, "The Birds Directive 15 Years Later: A Survey of the Case Law and a Comparison with the Habitats Directive" (1994) 6(2) *Journal of Environmental Law* 219

**Government publications and consultation papers**

*Biodiversity: The UK Action Plan* (1994) (Cm 2428 HMSO)

DETR (1999), *Access to Open Countryside in England and Wales*

DETR (1998), *Sites of Special Scientific Interest: Better Protection and Management*

*Sustainable Development - the UK Strategy* (1994) (Cm 2426 HMSO)

*Appendix A*

# Useful Names and
## · Addresses ·

English Nature
Northminster House
Peterborough
Cambridgeshire PE1 1UA
Tel: 01733 455000

Council for the Protection of
Rural England (CPRE)
Warwick House
25 Buckingham Palace Road
London SW1 OPP
Tel: (020) 7976 6433

Country Landowners
Association
16 Belgrave Square
London SW1X 8PQ
Tel: (020) 7235 0511

Countryside Agency
John Dower House
Crescent Place
Cheltenham GL50 3RA
Tel: 01242 521381

Department of the Environment,
Transport and the Regions
Eland House
Bressenden Place
London SW1E 5DU
Tel: (020) 7890 3000

Environment Agency
Hampton House
20 Albert Embankment
London SE1 7TJ
Tel: (020) 7820 5012

Friends of the Earth
26-28 Underwood Street
London N1 7JQ
Tel: (020) 7490 1555

Greenpeace
Canonbury Villas
London N1 2PN
Tel: (020) 7865 8100

Joint Nature Conservancy
Council
Monkstone House
City Road
Peterborough
Cambridgeshire PE1 1JY
Tel: 01733 62626

Ministry of Agriculture, Fisheries
and Food
Whitehall Place
London SW1A 2HH
Tel: (020) 7238 6000

National Farmers' Union (NFU)
22 Long Acre
Covent Garden
London WC2E 9LY
Tel: (020) 7331 7200

The Open Spaces Society
25A Bell Street
Henley-on-Thames
Oxon RG9 2BA
Tel: 01491 573535

The Ramblers' Association
1-5 Wandsworth Road
London SW8 2XX
Tel: (020) 7582 6878

The Royal Society for the
Protection of Birds (RSPB)
The Lodge
Sandy
Bedfordshire SG19 2DL
Tel: 01767 680551

Wildlife Trusts
The Green
Witham Park
Waterside
South Lincoln NG31 6LL
Tel: 01522 544400

*Appendix B*

# List of Potentially Damaging Operations

| Standard Ref No | Type of operation |
|---|---|
| 1 | Cultivation, including ploughing, rotovating, harrowing and re-seeding. |
| 2 | Changes in the grazing regime including type of stock, intensity or seasonal pattern of grazing and cessation of grazing. |
| 3 | The introduction of stock feeding and changes in stock feeding practice. |
| 4 | Changes in the mowing or cutting regime including hay making to silage and cessation. |
| 5 | Application of manure, fertilisers and lime. |
| 6 | Application of pesticides, including herbicides (weedkillers). |
| 7 | Dumping, spreading, or discharge of any materials. |
| 8 | Burning. |
| 9 | The release into the site of any wild, feral or domestic animal*, plant or seed. |
| 10 | The killing or removal of any wild animal*, other than pest control. |
| 11 | The destruction, displacement, removal or cutting of any plant or plant remains, including tree, shrub, herb, hedge, moss, lichen, fungus, and turf. |
| 12 | The introduction of tree and/or woodland management and changes in tree and/or woodland management including afforestation, planting, felling, coppicing and cessation of management. |
| 13a | Drainage including the use of mole, tile, tunnel or other artificial drains. |

14       The changing of water levels and tables and water utilisation including irrigation, storage and abstraction and through boreholes.

15       Infilling of ditches and drains.

20       Extraction of minerals, including sand and gravel, topsoil and subsoil.

21       Construction, removal or destruction of roads, tracks, walls, fences, hard-stands, banks, ditches or other earthworks, or the laying, maintenance or removal of pipelines and cables, above or below ground.

22       Storage of materials.

23       Erection of permanent or temporary structures, or the undertaking of engineering works, including drilling.

26       Use of vehicles likely to damage or disturb the meadows.

27       Recreational or other activities likely to damage the meadows.

28       Introduction of game or waterfowl management and changes in game and waterfowl management and hunting practice.

\* "animal" includes any mammal, reptile, amphibian, bird, fish or invertebrate.

*Appendix C*

# Consideration of · Development Proposals · Affecting SPAs and SACs

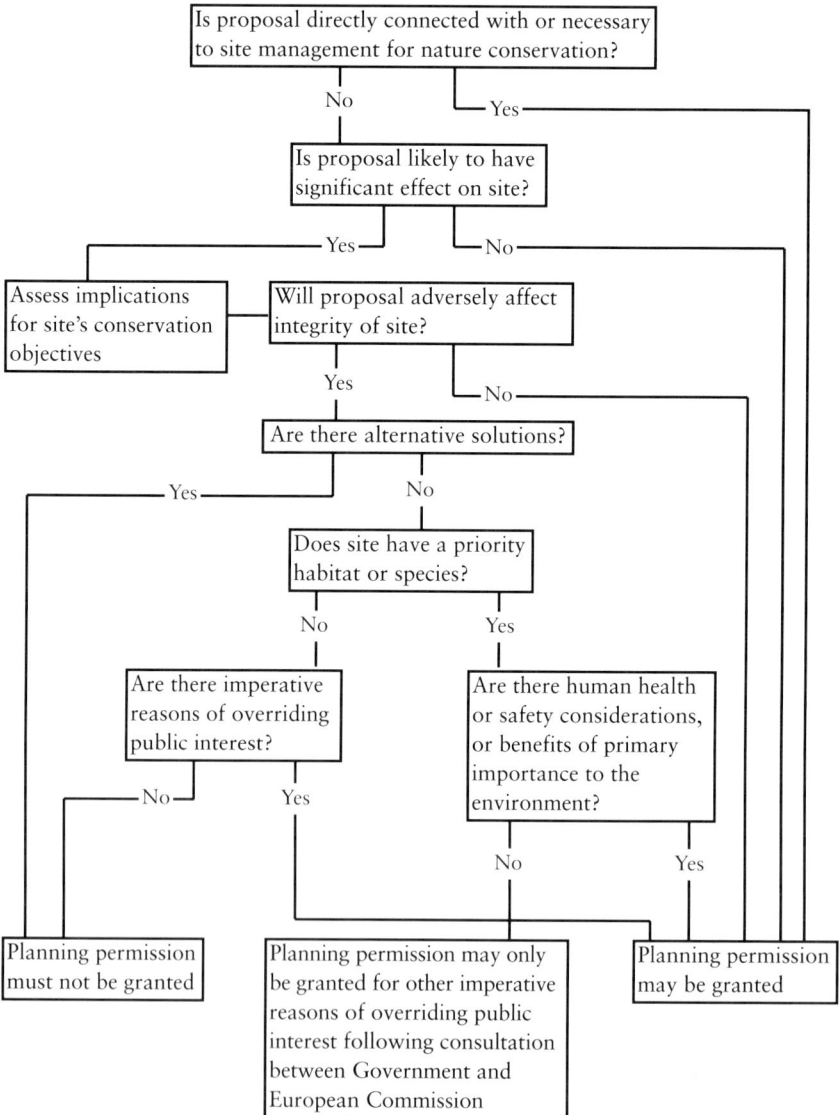

Is proposal directly connected with or necessary to site management for nature conservation?

No — Yes

Is proposal likely to have significant effect on site?

Yes — No

Assess implications for site's conservation objectives

Will proposal adversely affect integrity of site?

Yes — No

Are there alternative solutions?

Yes — No

Does site have a priority habitat or species?

No — Yes

Are there imperative reasons of overriding public interest?

No — Yes

Are there human health or safety considerations, or benefits of primary importance to the environment?

No — Yes

Planning permission must not be granted

Planning permission may only be granted for other imperative reasons of overriding public interest following consultation between Government and European Commission

Planning permission may be granted

## Appendix D

# Permitted Development Rights for SPAs and SACs

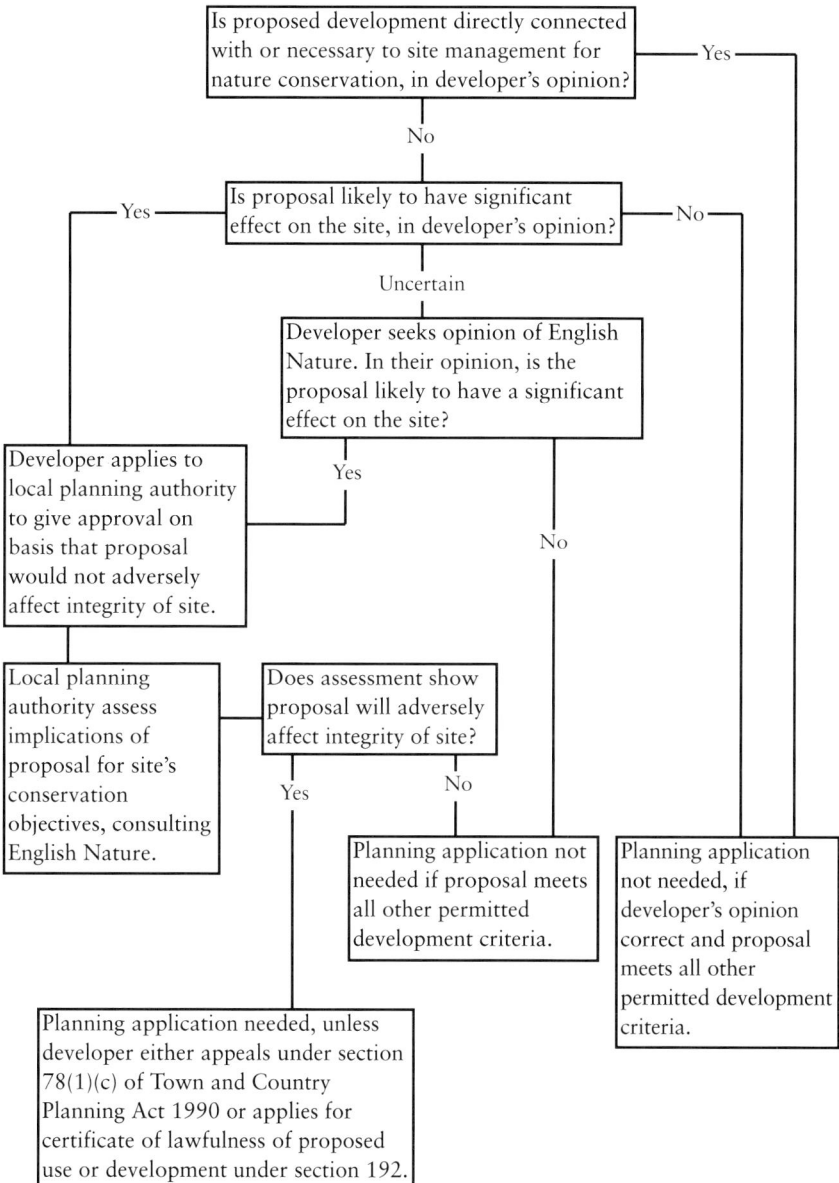

Is proposed development directly connected with or necessary to site management for nature conservation, in developer's opinion? ——— Yes ———

No

Is proposal likely to have significant effect on the site, in developer's opinion?

——— Yes ———   ——— No ———

Uncertain

Developer seeks opinion of English Nature. In their opinion, is the proposal likely to have a significant effect on the site?

Yes

No

Developer applies to local planning authority to give approval on basis that proposal would not adversely affect integrity of site.

Local planning authority assess implications of proposal for site's conservation objectives, consulting English Nature.

Does assessment show proposal will adversely affect integrity of site?

Yes   No

Planning application not needed if proposal meets all other permitted development criteria.

Planning application not needed, if developer's opinion correct and proposal meets all other permitted development criteria.

Planning application needed, unless developer either appeals under section 78(1)(c) of Town and Country Planning Act 1990 or applies for certificate of lawfulness of proposed use or development under section 192.

# · Hedgerow Removal Notice ·

*The Environment Act 1995*

*The Hedgerows Regulations 1997*

To: (Name and address of
local planning authority)

From: (Name and address of person giving the notice

1.   I give you notice under regulation 5(1)(a) of the above Regulations that I propose to remove the [stretch(es) of] hedgerow(s) indicated on the attached plan. *(If possible, please provide a plan to a scale of 1:2500. A different scale can be used so long as it shows clearly the location and length of the hedgerow or hedgerows that you wish to remove.)*

2.   The reasons why I propose to remove it/them are the following:—

3.   Of the [stretch(es) of] hedgerow(s) indicated, those marked with an "X" were planted less than 30 years ago. Evidence of the date of planting is attached.

4.   I am/We are the owner(s) of the freehold of the land concerned.

   OR (please delete as appropriate)
   I am/We are the tenant(s) of the agricultural holding concerned.

   OR (please delete as appropriate)
   I am/We are the tenant(s) under the farm business tenancy concerned.

   OR (please delete as appropriate)
   I am/act for the utility operator concerned.

(Signature of person giving notice)                    (Date)

## Appendix F

# · Hedgerow Retention Notice ·

*Hedgerow Removal Notice, OS [      ]*
*Removal of approximately 140 metres of hedgerow*
*Removal notice received by the District Planning Authority on  [       ]*

The removal of the hedgerow consisting of, or including, work specified in the removal notice in relation to the above hedgerow, is **PROHIBITED**

This prohibition is not time limited. It lasts until such time as:

- the hedgerow retention notice is withdrwn under regulation 5(8);
- the hedgerow retention notice is quashed under regulation 9(3)(b), as a result of a successful appeal
- a fresh removal notice is submitted, in response to which a retention notice is not issued

The above hedgerow is considered to be important for the following reason/s:

1.  The hedgerow marks part of the boundary of the historic parish of                    . The earliest maps in the County Record Office (dated 1740 and 1759) show the hedgerow as the boundary of the parish and manor of                and the parish of                    .

In reaching the decision to issue this Hedgerow Retention Notice this authority has had regard to your reasons for requesting the removal of the hedgerow, however, it is not satisfied that the particular circumstances of your application justify the removal of an important hedgerow. It is considered that there are other practicable ways in which to clean and maintain the neighbouring ditch without recourse to removing this important hedgerow.

*Rights of Appeal*

Regulation 9 of the above regulations provides a right of appeal against a Hedgerow Retention Notice. An appeal may be made in writing to the Secretary of State within 28 days of the date of this Notice, or such longer period as the Secretary of State may allow. Appeals must be made to the Department of Environment, Tollgate House, Houlton Street, Bristol BS2 9DJ.

The notice of appeal shall state the grounds for appeal. A copy of the notice of appeal shall be sent to the local planning authority which issued the Retention Notice.

Please note that the Hedgerow Retention Notice remains in force whilst any appeal is being considered.

*Note*

For your information advice on hedgerow management and the availability of grants may be available from:

Signed: —————————————
Date:   —————————————

*Appendix G*

# · Hedgerow Regulations 1997 ·

*Schedule 1*

## ADDITIONAL CRITERIA FOR DETERMINING "IMPORTANT" HEDGEROWS

PART I   INTERPRETATION

In this Schedule—

"building" includes Structure;

"Record Office" means—

(a) a place appointed under section 4 of the Public Records Act 1958 (place of deposit of public records),

(b) a place at which documents are held pursuant to a transfer under section 144A(4) of the Law of Property Act 1922 or under section 36(2) of the Tithe Act 1936, including each of those provisions as applied by section 7(1) of the Local Government (Records) Act 1962, or

(c) a place at which documents are made available for inspection by a local authority pursuant to section 1 of the Local Government (Records) Act 1962;

"relevant date" means the date on which these Regulations are made;

"Sites and Monuments Record" means a record of archaeological features and sites adopted—

(a) by resolution of a local authority within the meaning of the Local Government Act 1972, or

(b) in Greater London, by the Historic Buildings and Monuments Commission;

"standard tree"

(a) in the case of a multi-stemmed tree, means a tree which, when measured at a point 1.3 metres from natural ground level, has a least two stems whose diameters are at least 15 centimetres;

(b) in the case of a single-stemmed tree, means a tree which, when measured at a point 1.3 metres from natural ground level, has a stems whose diameter is at least 20 centimetres;

"woodland species" means the species listed in Schedule 2; and

"woody species" means the species and sub-species listed in Schedule 3, and any hybrid, that is to say any individual plant resulting from a cross between parents of any species or sub-species so listed, but does not include any cultivar; and references to the documents in paragraph 6(3)(b) and (4) are to those documents as a the relevant date, without taking account of any subsequent revisions, supplements or modifications.

PART II　CRITERIA

**Archaeology and history**

1.　The hedgerow marks the boundary or part of the boundary, of at least one historic parish or township; and for this purpose "historic" means existing before 1850.

2.　The hedgerow incorporates an archaeological feature which is—
    (a) included in the schedule of monuments complied by the Secretary of State under section 1 (schedule of monuments) of the Ancient Monuments and Archaeological Areas Act 1979; or
    (b) recorded at the relevant date in a Sites and Monuments Record.

3.　The hedgerow—
    (a) is situated wholly or partly within an archaeological site included or recorded as mentioned in paragraph 2 or on land adjacent to and associated with such a site; and
    (b) is associated with any monument or feature on that site.

4.　The hedgerow—
    (a) marks the boundary of a pre-1600 AD estate or manor recorded at the relevant date in a Sites and Monuments Record or in a document held at that date at a Record Office; or
    (b) is visibly related to any building or other feature of such an estate or manor.

5.　The hedgerow—
    (a) is recorded in a document held at the relevant date at a Record Office as an integral part of a field system pre-dating the Inclosure Acts; or
    (b) is part of, or visibly related to, any building or other feature associated with such a system, and that system—
        (i) is substantially complete; or
        (ii) is of a pattern which is recorded in a document prepared before the relevant date by a local planning authority, within the meaning of the 1990 Act, for the purposes of development control within the authority's area, as a key landscape characteristic.

**Wildlife and landscape**

6.—(1)　The hedgerow—
    (a) contains species listed or categorised as mentioned in sub-paragraph (3); or
    (b) is referred to in a record held immediately before the relevant date by a biological record centre maintained by, or on behalf of, a local authority within the meaning of the Local Government Act 1972, and

in a form recognised by the Nature Conservancy Council for England, the Countryside Council for Wales or the Joint Nature Conservation Committee, as having contained any such species—

(i) in the case of animals and birds, subject to sub-paragraph (2), within the period of five years immediately before the relevant date,

(ii) in the case of plants, subject of sub-paragraph (2), within the period of ten years immediately before the relevant date;

(2) Where more than one record referable to the period of five or as the case may be, ten years before the relevant date is held by a particular biological record centre, and the more (or most) recent record does not satisfy the criterion specified in sub-paragraph (1)(b), the criterion is not satisfied(notwithstanding that an earlier record satisfies it).

(3) The species referred to in sub-paragraph (1) are those—

(a) listed in Part I (protection at all times) of Schedule 1 (birds which are protected by special penalties), Schedule 5 (animals which are protected) or Schedule 8 (plants which are protected) to the Wildlife and Countryside Act 1981;

(b) categorised as a declining breeder (category 3) in "Red Data Birds in Britain" Batten LA, Libby CJ, Clement P, Elliott GD and Porter RF (Eds.), published in 1990 for the Nature Conservancy Council and the Royal Society for the Protection of Birds (ISBN 0 855661 056 9): or

(c) categorised as "endangered", "extinct", "rare" or "vulnerable" in Britain in a document mentioned in sub-paragraph (4).

(4) The documents referred to in sub-paragraph (3)(c) are—

(a) of the books known as the British Red Data Books:

1. "Vascular Plants" Perring FH and Farrell L, 2nd Edition, published in 1983 for the Royal Society for Nature Conservation (ISBN 0 902484 04 4);

2. "Insects" Shirt DB (Ed.), published in 1987 for the Nature Conservancy Council (ISBN 0 86139 380 5); and

3. "Invertebrates other than insects" Bratton JH (Ed.), published in 1991 for the Joint Nature Conservation Committee (ISBN 1 873701 00 4); and

(b) of the books known as the Red Data Books of Britain and Ireland: "Stonewarts" Stewart NF and Church JM, published in 1992 for the Joint Nature Conservation Committee (ISBN 1 873701 24 1).

7.—(1) Subject to sub-paragraph (2), the hedgerow includes—

(a) at least 7 woody species;

(b) at least 6 woody species, and has associated with it at least 3 of the features specified in sub-paragraph (4);

(c) at least 6 woody species, including one of the following—
black-poplar tree (*Populus nigra ssp betulifolia*);

large leaved lime (*Tilia platyphyllos*);

small-leaved lime (*Tillia cordata*);

wild service tree (*Sorbus torminalis*); or

(d) at least 5 woody species, and has associated with it at least 4 of the
features specified in sub-paragraph (4),

and the number of woody species in a hedgerow shall be ascertained in
accordance with sub-paragraph (3).

(2) Where the hedgerow in question is situated wholly or partly in the
county (as constituted on 1st April 1997) of the City of Kingston upon Hull,
Cumbria, Darlington, Durham, East Riding of Yorkshire, Hartlepool,
Lancashire, Middlesborough, North East Lincolnshire, North Lincolnshire,
Northumberland, North Yorkshire, Redcar and Cleveland, Stockton-on-Tees,
Tyne and Wear, West Yorkshire or York, the number of woody species
mentioned in paragraphs (a) to (d) of sub-paragraph (1) is to be treated as
reduced by one.

(3)  For the purposes of sub-paragraph (I) (and those of paragraph 8(b))—

(a) where the length of the hedgerow does not exceed 30 metres, count
the number of woody species present in the hedgerow;

(b) where the length of the hedgerow exceeds 30 metres, but does not
exceed 100 metres, count the number of woody species present in the
central stretch of 30 metres;

(c) where the length of the hedgerow exceeds 100 metres, but does not
exceed 200 metres, count the number of woody species present in the
central stretch of 30 metres within each half of the hedgerow and
divide the aggregate by two;

(d) where the length of the hedgerow exceeds 200 metres, count the
number of woody species present in the central stretch of 30 metres
within each third of the hedgerow and divide the aggregate by three.

(4)  The features referred to in sub-paragraph (1)(b) and (d) (which include
those referred to in paragraph 8(b) are —

(a) a bank or wall which supports the hedgerow along at least one half of
its length;

(b) gaps which in aggregate do not exceed 10 per cent of the length of the
hedgerow;

(c) where the length of the hedgerow does not exceed 50 metres, at least
one standard tree;

(d) where the length of the hedgerow exceeds 50 metres but does not
exceed 100 metres, at least 2 standard trees;

(e) where the length of the hedgerow exceeds 100 metres, such number of
standard trees (within any part of its length) as would when averaged
over its total length amount to at least one for each 50 metres;

(f) at least 3 woodland species within one metre, in any direction, of the
outermost edges of the hedgerow;

(g) a ditch along at least one half of the length of the hedgerow;

(h) connections scoring 4 points or more in accordance with sub-paragraph (5);

(i) a parallel hedge within 15 metres of the hedgerow.

(5) For the purposes of sub-paragraph (4)(h) a connection with another hedgerow scores one point and a connection with a pond or a woodland in which the majority of trees are broad-leaved trees scores 2 points; and a hedgerow is connected with something not only if it meets it but also if it has a point within 10 metres of it and would meet it if the line of the hedgerow continued.

(8) The hedgerow—

(a) is adjacent to a bridleway or footpath, within the meaning of the Highways Act 1980, a road used as a public path, within the meaning of section 54 (duty to reclassify roads used as public paths) of the Wildlife and Countryside Act 1981, or a byway open to all traffic, within the meaning of Part III of the Wildlife and Countryside Act 1981 and

(b) includes at least 4 woody species, ascertained in accordance with paragraph 7(3) and at least 2 of the features specified in paragraph 7(4)(a) to (g).

# · Index ·